IMAGES OF WAR

ARMOURED WARFARE AND THE WAFFEN SS 1944–1945

Leibstandarte Panzer IV Ausf F2 in occupied France.

IMAGES OF WAR

ARMOURED WARFARE AND THE WAFFEN SS 1944–1945

RARE PHOTOGRAPHS FROM WARTIME ARCHIVES

Anthony Tucker-Jones

Pen & Sword
MILITARY

First published in Great Britain in 2017 by
PEN & SWORD MILITARY
an imprint of
Pen & Sword Books Ltd,
47 Church Street,
Barnsley,
South Yorkshire
S70 2AS

A CIP record for this book is available from the British Library.

ISBN 978 1 47387 794 8

Typeset by CHIC GRAPHICS

Printed and bound by CPI Group (UK) Ltd, Croydon, CR0 4YY

Pen & Sword Books Ltd incorporates the imprints of Pen & Sword Archaeology, Atlas, Aviation, Battleground, Discovery, Family History, History, Maritime, Military, Naval, Politics, Railways, Select, Social History, Transport, True Crime, Claymore Press, Frontline Books, Leo Cooper, Praetorian Press, Remember When, Seaforth Publishing and Wharncliffe.

For a complete list of Pen & Sword titles please contact
Pen & Sword Books Limited
47 Church Street, Barnsley, South Yorkshire, S70 2AS, England
E-mail: enquiries@pen-and-sword.co.uk
Website: www.pen-and-sword.co.uk

Contents

Introduction: Hitler's Armoured Bodyguard

The focus of this book is purely the main armoured operations of the Waffen-SS during the latter half of the Second World War. It offers a graphic snapshot of the dramatic tank battles fought by the Waffen-SS panzer and panzergrenadier divisions during 1944–1945 on both the Eastern and Western Fronts. By this stage these units were at the height of their powers and were involved in major operations in France, Russia, the Netherlands, Poland and Germany. Most notably the Waffen-SS's panzers prolonged the war by staving off defeat, briefly stabilising both the Eastern and Western Fronts at highly critical points in the fighting.

It is worth highlighting that Reichsführer-SS Heinrich Himmler's Schutz-Staffel (SS) had a huge variety of units with differing functions. The front-line combat troops of the Waffen-SS (Armed SS), with their grey uniforms, should not be confused with the men of the Allgemeine-SS (General SS), with their distinctive ceremonial black uniforms, who were the 'general service' militia of the Nazi Party. The latter over the years came to epitomise the SS but they were a separate entity from the Waffen-SS.

Similarly, the Sicherheitsdienst (SD – Security Service) security police wore grey, while the Gestapo secret police worked in plain clothes. In addition, the SS-Totenkopfverbände (Death's Head Units) responsible for running the concentration camps in Poland and Russia also dressed in field-grey uniforms. The latter oversaw Hitler's Final Solution and the wholesale murder of Europe's Jewish population. Then there was a vast range of other police and security units raised within occupied Europe and controlled by the SS.

Over the years the Waffen-SS has been elevated to a largely undeserved elite status by a series of military historians. The result is that its units are often mentioned in the same breath as Spartan hoplites, Persian immortals, Roman Praetorian Guard, Vikings, Japanese Samurai, Delta Force and the SAS, to name but a few. This reputation is mainly derived from the performance of a handful of tough SS panzer divisions that fought on the Eastern and Western Fronts with, it has to be said, some distinction.

In fact, many of these divisions consisted of little more than boy soldiers recruited from the *Hitlerjugend* (Hitler Youth) and the Reich Labour Service. While some of the early Waffen-SS field units proved consistently reliable, this was as a result of a selection and training process deeply rooted in Nazi ideology. This politically motivated fanaticism spilled over into their conduct and regularly resulted in wholly unjustifiable war crimes and atrocities.

The Waffen-SS grew from the *SS-Verfügungstruppen* (SS-VT – SS Dispositional Troops), the military wing of the Schutz-Staffel – the Führer's personal protection squad. Ironically, after his experiences with the powerful pre-war Sturmabteilung (SA: Storm Detachment) of the National Socialist German Workers' Party (NSDAP or Nazi Party), Adolf Hitler was not in favour of large private armies. However, the SS was used to decapitate and take control of the SA, ensuring it posed no threat to Hitler's steady rise to power.

The deployment of SS units during the invasions of Poland and the West were simply designed to allow Reichsführer-SS Himmler's power base to share in Germany's military triumphs. Himmler had assumed control of the SS in 1929 and immediately set about empire building. The premier formation, *Leibstandarte-SS Adolf Hitler*, evolved from Hitler's pre-war bodyguard commanded by 'Sepp' Dietrich. Likewise *Das Reich*, formerly the SS-VT Division, evolved from the remainder of the pre-war armed SS. From these units grew Himmler's autonomous army of over half a million men, fully equipped with tanks and artillery.

In total, the Waffen-SS, a very distinct and independent entity from the regular German Army, raised (on paper at least) a total of thirty-eight divisions during the Second World War. Of these, seven were panzer divisions and another eight were panzergrenadier divisions. The most famous – or perhaps infamous – armoured formations were the 1st SS *Leibstandarte-SS Adolf Hitler*, the 2nd SS *Das Reich* and the 12th SS *Hitlerjugend*. The 5th SS *Wiking*, the 9th *Hohenstaufen* and the 10th SS *Frundsberg* also gained reputations as fierce and brutal fighters. The least well known was the 3rd SS *Totenkopf*, which was initially raised from concentration camp guards.

The panzergrenadier divisions comprised the 4th SS *Polizei*, the 16th SS *Reichsführer-SS*, which gained an unsavoury reputation in Italy, the 11th SS *Nordland*, the 17th SS *Götz von Berlichingen* which fought in Normandy, the 18th SS *Horst Wessel*, the 23rd SS *Nederland*, the 28th SS *Wallonien* and the 38th SS *Nibelungen*. The latter was recruited from teenage SS cadets in March 1945 and never even reached regimental size. Most of these units included single panzer and assault gun battalions.

The emergence of Himmler's panzer divisions was not just a political vanity project; there were sound strategic reasons for upgrading them from the early motorised units. The expansion of German strength in 1943 had clearly accelerated after Rommel's defeat at El Alamein in November 1942, the Allied landings in French North Africa that same month and by the destruction in early 1943 of the German forces trapped at Stalingrad. *Liebstandarte-SS Adolf Hitler*, *Das Reich* and *Totenkopf* were transformed into panzergrenadier units for the spring 1943 counter-offensive in the Soviet Union, each with an integral tank battalion. This increase in combat power had been authorised in early 1942 but was not implemented until the second half of the year. Notably, the *Wiking* division was also allocated a tank battalion but stayed in the line instead of being withdrawn to France to re-equip.

Equally important was the appointment of General Heinz Guderian as Inspector-General of Armoured Troops in February 1943. Answering directly to Hitler, he was responsible for recruiting, training, organising and equipping the panzer divisions of both the regular German Army and the Waffen-SS. Working alongside Armaments Minister Albert Speer, Guderian concentrated on centralising weapons production. This put an end to the private industries the SS had created in the face of the army's intransigence over supplying modern equipment.

The result of this was that the armoured Waffen-SS divisions began to be given priority with new tanks and self-propelled guns. When the fully fledged SS panzer divisions appeared in 1943–1944 they had stronger tank establishments than their army counterparts. They also had priority with the new Tiger and Panther tanks when they appeared, even though these were in short supply.

By 1944 a Waffen-SS panzer division consisted of up to 15,000 fighting men and up to 6,000 support personnel, such as administrative staff, clerks and medics. The basic organisation comprised a panzer regiment, two panzergrenadier regiments and a panzer artillery regiment, plus anti-tank, assault gun, flak, pioneer, reconnaissance and signals battalions. Each SS panzer regiment had an established strength of up to 2,000 men. It consisted of two battalions, each with four companies, with an average of fifteen panzers (Mk IVs and Vs) per company. The regiment was also issued with about a dozen self-propelled anti-aircraft guns equipped with Möbelwagens, Wirbelwinds or Ostwinds. The latter had become an increasing necessity in light of the waning power of the Luftwaffe. In addition, there was a supporting pioneer company, plus up to 400 motorcycles, cars and trucks.

In comparison, the assault gun battalions were rather weak, being issued with about twenty StuG III/IVs in three companies totalling just 300 personnel. The anti-tank or panzerjäger battalions had three companies, two of which had fifteen self-propelled tank destroyers; these were normally Jagdpanzer IVs. The third company was armed with towed 75mm PaK40 anti-tank guns. The reconnaissance and pioneer battalions were stronger, with almost 1,000 men. Notably, the reconnaissance units were equipped with a dozen 75mm self-propelled guns (usually mounted in armoured cars for mobility) and had integral anti-tank and anti-aircraft guns. Such forces proved a scourge for the Alllies at Arnhem and Nijmegen.

The mechanised armoured infantry or panzergrenadier regiments were normally organised into three battalions plus supporting units numbering up to 4,000 personnel. Each had five companies equipped with SdKfz 251 armoured half-tracks. For mobile fire support they had six 150mm self-propelled Hummels and twelve 105mm self-propelled Wespes, plus twenty-four flamethrower vehicles and twelve 120mm mortar carriers. The anti-aircraft battalions were formed from five companies, three 20mm light and two 88mm heavy, each with six guns.

An SS panzer artillery regiment comprised twelve batteries in four battalions. One battery in each battalion was equipped with self-propelled guns, whilst the rest were towed weapons. From September 1944 Nebelwerfer rocket launcher battalions were added to SS panzer divisions. Each had four companies, three with 150mm weapons and one with 210mm weapons. These were either on wheeled trailers or mounted on half-tracks.

Although the powerful Tiger I and II tanks fought alongside the SS panzer divisions, they did not form part of the divisional organisation and were formed into three independent Heavy (Schwere) panzer battalions. In 1944 the 1st SS Panzer Corps in the West was allocated Schwere SS Panzer Abteilung 101 as its Tiger I battalion. The Tigers bore crossed keys within a shield with flanking oakleaves insignia to reflect their links with *Leibstandarte*, although they fought with *Hitlerjugend*. Schwere SS Panzer Abteilung 102 was assigned to support the 2nd SS Panzer Corps, while 103 was sent to the Eastern Front as part of the 3rd (Germanic) SS Panzer Corps.

The subsequent Tiger II was then allotted to Schwere Panzer Abteilungen 501 (formerly 101), 502 (102) and 503 (103); these tanks were similarly considered corps level assets and deployed at divisional level as and when they were needed. 501 took part in the Ardennes offensive, 502 was destroyed in the defence of Berlin and 503, after fighting alongside *Nordland*, surrendered after being decimated in East Prussia.

What really made the Waffen-SS visually distinctive and therefore perhaps brought them more notice than they deserved was their disruptive pattern camouflaged smocks and helmet covers. There were four basic patterns, all reversible. The Waffen-SS employed spots while the regular army and the Luftwaffe used patterns of angular segments. The Waffen-SS units were also issued with M43 and M44 camouflaged uniforms that consisted of jackets and trousers. The tank and self-propelled gun crews wore one-piece non-reversible camouflage overalls during the latter half of the war.

It is important to highlight that Reichsführer-SS Heinrich Himmler was not a military man but a civilian, despite wearing a uniform. Unlike many of his Nazi contemporaries, he was not a veteran of the First World War. His main ability was choosing skilled subordinates who made the SS look good. In addition, he was a highly efficient administrator.

While the Waffen-SS on the whole proved to be a highly competent fighting machine, Himmler by contrast had no flair for military operations. Towards the end of the Second World War he was appointed to command Army Group Upper Rhine and then Army Group Vistula. Both roles required skills far beyond his abilities and both commands were short-lived. Indeed, placing him in charge of Army Group Upper Rhine was a political move to keep him away from Hitler's Ardennes offensive, which involved the SS panzer divisions. In the case of Army Group Vistula, Himmler was not only removed but also beforehand was prevented from directing Operation Solstice.

Once manpower became an issue, Himmler was increasingly forced to rely on 'ethnic' Germans and foreign 'volunteers' from the occupied territories. At this point quality and discipline often became an issue. The better known mixed-nationality foreign units, such as the Danish and Dutch 5th SS Panzer Division *Wiking*, the Austrian and Romanian 7th SS Freiwilligen Gebirgs Division *Prince Eugen*, the Austrian and Slovenian 16th SS Panzergrenadier Division *Reichsführer-SS* and the Belgian 28th SS Panzergrenadier Division *Wallonien*, were all equipped with armoured fighting vehicles.

The so-called Waffen-SS foreign 'volunteer' cavalry, grenadier, mountain and panzergrenadier divisions were a motley crew, many of whom were of extremely dubious fighting value. Most were employed in security duties and anti-partisan sweeps which frequently resulted in the deaths of innocent civilians. Considerable elements of the SS were morally bankrupt, representing an organisation that had little regard for humanity, and committed some of the worst atrocities in history. The SS Einsatzgruppen and concentration camp guards were the main culprits, but the Waffen-SS combat divisions were also guilty of such crimes. Tough fighting men, they were responsible for a whole series of massacres carried out across Europe. The worst of these was perpetrated during the Warsaw Rising in 1944, when the SS murdered tens of thousands of civilians.

War crimes and politics aside, Hitler's SS panzer divisions proved particularly adept at conducting rescue and defensive operations, and Hitler became increasingly reliant on the Waffen-SS to extricate his armed forces from tricky military situations. Their finest moments during 1944–1945 came at Arnhem, Wolomin and the Ardennes, where significant Allied advances were stopped dead by a handful of veteran Waffen-SS divisions. The German Army greatly respected the Waffen-SS panzer divisions and fought side by side with them, until they became largely one and the same.

As the war came to a close, it became apparent that the Waffen-SS's once impressive offensive capability had been all but exhausted, though morale never waned or crumbled. At the very end they were the main strike force for Hitler's final counter-offensives in Belgium and Hungary. When the Waffen-SS failed to secure a victory or come to the rescue of Berlin, Hitler felt personally betrayed by them. One of his final futile gestures was to order them to remove their SS insignia.

* * *

Photograph Sources

All photographs in this book are sourced via the author.

Reichsführer Heinrich Himmler created the Waffen-SS from Hitler's personal protection squad. It grew to include fourteen panzer and panzergrenadier divisions. Lacking military experience, Himmler surrounded himself with highly able generals.

Chapter One

Himmler's SS Panzer Divisions

The 1st SS Panzer Division *Leibstandarte-SS Adolf Hitler* dated back to 1925 and the creation of Hitler's SS protection squad, building on the Nazi's short-lived Sturmabteilung (SA) *Stabswache* (Headquarters Guard). In March 1933 Joseph 'Sepp' Dietrich established the *SS-Stabswache Berlin*, consisting of 120 men, who, along with the *SS-Verfügungstruppe*, were the forerunners of the Waffen-SS. Initially the unit was based at Berlin's Alexander Barracks but later moved to Berlin-Lichterfelde.

The *SS-Stabswache Berlin* was redesignated *SS-Sonderkommando Zossen* and in September 1933 merged with the newly raised *SS-Sonderkommando Jüterbog* to form the *SS-Leibstandarte (Bodyguard) Adolf Hitler* (LAH). The following year it was redesignated as the *Leibstandarte-SS Adolf Hitler* (LSSAH) and grew to regimental strength.

The LSSAH took part in the Austrian Anschluss as part of 16th Corps under General Heinz Guderian and later in the annexation of Czechoslovakia. During the invasion of Poland it served with Army Group South under the leadership of SS-Oberstgruppenführer 'Sepp' Dietrich and later took part in the invasion of France and the Low Countries, where it was mainly held in reserve, although it saw some action against the retreating British troops at Dunkirk. The LSSAH was attached to 14th Corps during the second and final phase of the invasion of France.

Formed in October 1939 from the *Deutschland*, *Germania* and *Der Führer* Regiments, the SS-VT-Division *Reich* was placed under the command of SS-Oberstgruppenführer Paul Hausser. It was also involved in the campaign in the West in 1940 and after a period spent guarding the border with Vichy France was transferred to the Netherlands. The division then took part in the campaign in the Balkans, where a small detachment led by SS-Hauptsturmführer Klingenberg managed to get the Mayor of Belgrade to surrender the city without a fight.

Still under the command of Hausser, SS-VT-Division *Reich* took part in the invasion of the Soviet Union and fought on the front line until August 1941, when it was withdrawn for refitting. It was sent back to the front in September and a few months later, commanded by SS-Obergruppenführer Wilhelm 'Willi' Bittrich, it took part in the failed winter offensive against Moscow.

The idea to create a Hitler Youth or *Hitlerjugend* division was initially suggested by Gruppenführer Gottlob Berger in early 1943. His plan envisaged the drafting of all 17-year-old Hitler Youth members born in 1926 and assigning them to a combat formation. Hitler liked the proposal and ordered Berger to commence organising such a division, the official order being issued on 10 February 1943.

Berger nominated himself to be the first *Hitlerjugend* divisional commander, but Himmler gave the job instead to a former Hitler Youth member, Oberführer Fritz Witt, as he had been commanding one of the 1st SS Panzer Division's panzergrenadier regiments. Witt had won the Iron Cross and Knight's Cross in Poland and France respectively. In the Balkans his men from the 1st SS were instrumental in opening the Klidi pass to the heart of Greece. He then fought in Russia, seeing action at Rostov and Kharkov.

Hitler issued a number of additional decrees in April 1943 regarding the formation of the *Hitlerjugend* Panzergrenadier Division. On 1 May the first batch of 8,000 volunteers reported for six weeks' training, although in the event they only received four. At the beginning of July the graduating class was released for service, while a second batch of 8,000 was inducted for training. By 1 September 1943 the 16,000 trained recruits were listed on the rosters of the newly formed *Hitlerjugend* Division and were assembled at an SS training facility located at Beverloo, Belgium.

Under the direction of 'Willi' Bittrich, the 9th SS Panzer Division *Hohenstaufen* was also formed in early February 1943, mainly from conscripts, many of them from the *Reichsarbeitsdienst* (RAD or Reich Labour Service). Bittrich, an able tank commander, controlled the *Deutschland* Regiment during the fighting in Poland and France in 1939–1940; he then assumed control of the 2nd SS Panzer Division *Das Reich* for just three months in late 1941.

Under the command of SS-Standartenführer Michael Lippert, the 10th SS Panzer Division, like the 9th SS, was raised in February 1943 from conscripts drawn mainly from the *Reichsarbeitsdienst*. Again they were just teenagers; according to Himmler, the average age of the recruits was 18 years old. The division was redesignated the 10th SS Panzer Division on 3 October 1943 and named after Georg von Frundsberg (1473–1528), who had served the Hapsburg Monarchy during its many wars.

The LSSAH was upgraded to brigade strength in August 1940 for the planned invasion of Britain. When this was called off, the LSSAH was transferred to Romania for the attack in the Balkans. Its troops fought their way through Yugoslavia and

Greece, chasing the Allied troops to Kalamata, from where they took flight by sea to Crete. Kurt Meyer, commanding *Liebstandarte*'s reconnaissance battalion, attacked the Klussura Pass and captured some 11,000 men; the LSSAH as a whole took the surrender of at least sixteen divisions before the Greeks capitulated.

In June 1941 the LSSAH, expanded into a full motorised infantry division, took part in the invasion of the Soviet Union as part of Army Group South and was involved in the fighting at Kiev and Rostov. The division was sent to France for refit in 1942 and upgraded to a panzergrenadier division. Sent back to the Eastern Front in 1943 under SS-Brigadeführer Theodor Wisch, it fought at Kharkov and Kursk. After the German defeat at Kursk, the LSSAH was sent to Italy on anti-partisan duties, but it was soon deployed back to the Eastern Front as a panzer division.

After suffering heavy losses on the Eastern Front, on 18 April 1944 the remains of the 1st SS under Wisch were sent by train to northwest France and established its headquarters at Turnhout in Belgium, where it became part of the 1st SS Panzer Corps. More than 2,000 men from the 12th SS were transferred to the division and in early May Hitler ordered that it should get new equipment, much of it straight from the factory floor.

A month later the 1st SS was still far from combat ready. In the week before D-Day the division stood at 19,620 strong, although many of the new recruits were untrained and more than 1,000 men, mainly drivers and vital technicians, were still in Germany. Wisch was still awaiting replacement Panzer Mk IVs and Vs and these did not arrive until the weeks after D-Day. Motor transport was lacking: the division had less than half its authorised number of trucks and more than a third of those they did have required maintenance. None of the panzergrenadiers' armoured half-tracks was operational.

The SS-VT-Division *Reich* was sent to France in March 1942, with the exception of a small Kampfgruppe, where it was upgraded to become SS Panzergrenadier Division *Das Reich*. It was sent back to the Eastern Front in January 1943, where, under the leadership of SS-Obergruppenführer George Keppler, it took part in the capture and recapture of Kharkov, as well as fighting at Kursk.

In April 1944, under SS-Gruppenführer Heinz Lammerding, some 2,500 men from *Das Reich* were transferred back to the Bordeaux area in France, this time to be upgraded to a full panzer division designated the 2nd SS. Lammerding had served as an infantry officer and was involved in anti-partisan operations on the Eastern Front. The subsequent actions of his division during its march north through France may be partly attributed to Lammerding's brutal experiences in the East.

In late 1943 Lammerding took command of those 2nd SS units on anti-partisan duties and on 25 January 1944 assumed full command of the division, based around Montauban. There were whisperings that he had been over-promoted. It has been argued that he owed his appointment to his relationship with Himmler, and indeed it was felt that Lammerding's position had more to do with his political allegiance to the Nazi Party rather than any real military aptitude. One of his first priorities was to absorb about 9,000 new recruits, as well as replenish his vehicle fleet. On 16 May 1944 the division took receipt of fifty-five Panzer IVs and thirty-seven Panthers towards a complement of sixty-two of each, to supplement the existing thirty Sturmgeschütz. By 10 June 1944 Lammerding found his command scattered across the Lot, Corrèze and Haute-Vienne, with broken-down panzers and StuGs dotted about between Tulle and Montauban. Frustratingly for Lammerding and his men, the actions of the French Maquis ensured that what should have been a three-day journey to Normandy took the 2nd SS a fortnight. The situation came to a head at Oradour-sur-Glane, 12 miles northwest of Limoges, where 646 people were killed by members of Panzergrenadier Regiment *Der Führer* under Sturmbannführer Otto Diekmann. (Diekmann would be killed in action on 30 June.)

Before the 9th SS had finished training, it was placed under 'Sepp' Dietrich's 1st SS Panzer Corps, along with the remains of the 1st SS and the newly raised 12th SS Panzergrenadier Division. However, in early 1944, along with the 10th SS, Panzer Lehr and the 349th Infantry Divisions, it became part of 2nd SS Panzer Corps under Paul Hausser. At the end of March 1944 the Red Army had surrounded the 1st Panzer Army and 2nd Panzer Corps had been despatched to rescue it.

The 9th SS first saw action in early 1944 at Tarnopol, where it took part in rescuing German troops from the Kamenets-Podolskiy pocket. Placed into reserve with Army Group North in Ukraine, the 9th SS was refitting when the Allies landed in Normandy. Hitler immediately ordered the division to join Panzergruppe West. Under Bittrich, it was sent to Normandy on 12 June, though it was to have a series of commanders during the Normandy campaign.

Led by SS-Gruppenführer Karl Fischer von Treuenfeld, the 10th SS Panzer Division likewise first saw action at Tarnopol. In mid-June Hitler ordered the division to be switched to the West to help bolster the situation in Normandy. Under SS-Gruppenführer Heinz Harmel it was sent to France on 12 June, along with the 9th SS, to counter the Allied landings.

On 1 June 1944, on paper at least, the 12th SS *Hitlerjugend* was an extremely powerful armoured formation with a reported strength of 20,500 men; however, some 2,400 of these troops were stationed at Arnhem in the Netherlands. It has been estimated that the 12th SS arrived in Normandy with about 17,000 men. SS Panzer Regiment 12, under SS-Obersturmbannführer Max Wünche, had an authorised strength of 101 Panzer IVs and 79 Panthers. A further thirteen Panthers were despatched to the division the day after D-Day.

Josef 'Sepp' Dietrich seen here as an SS-Obergruppenführer. He is wearing the Knight's Cross with Oakleaves and Swords. Dietrich was one of the Waffen-SS's most highly decorated soldiers and was only one of two to gain the Oakleaves with Swords and Diamonds. He helped Himmler create the Waffen-SS, first commanding the *Leibstandarte-SS Adolf Hitler*.

SS-Obergruppenführer Paul Hausser was another of the most successful generals in the Waffen-SS. He started the war commanding the SS-VT Division *Reich*. Hausser was one of the few SS generals prepared to disobey Hitler.

Hitler in Nürnberg in 1935 with the brown shirt SA to the left and black-clad SS to the right. That year field-grey uniforms the same as the black service uniform were issued to members of the *Leibstandarte-SS Adolf Hitler* and SS-VT for everyday wear.

Waffen-SS troops of the *Leibstandarte* being awarded Iron Crosses by 'Sepp' Dietrich in the summer of 1940. Hitler allowed Himmler's forces to share in Germany's early military victories.

Men of the *Leibstandarte-SS Adolf Hitler* involved in the invasion of the Balkans in early 1941. As a motorised infantry division, it took part in the attack on the Soviet Union that summer. It was then progressively upgraded from a panzergrenadier to a panzer division.

Waffen-SS soldiers act as a ceremonial guard for one of their dead comrades lost during the invasion of Poland in the summer of 1939. Note the SS runes on their collars.

Members of a Waffen-SS unit. The initial divisions started life as motorised infantry divisions and were steadily upgraded to panzergrenadier and then full panzer divisions during 1943–1944.

What made the Waffen-SS visually distinctive was their ground-breaking disruptive pattern camouflaged smocks and helmet covers. There were four basic patterns that were all reversible. The Waffen-SS was also issued with M1943 and M1944 camouflaged uniforms that consisted of jackets and trousers.

Mounted Waffen-SS troops in camouflaged smocks. The invasion of the Soviet Union triggered the rapid expansion of the Waffen-SS, including the 8th SS Cavalry Division Florian Geyer, which was destroyed during the fighting for Budapest in 1945.

This Panzer IV Ausf F2 belonging to the 1st SS Panzer Division was photographed in occupied France in the summer of 1942, shortly after the division was issued with this upgunned variant. Note the lack of camouflage at this stage of the war; the vehicle is painted in *dunkel grau* (panzer grey), which was the standard colour at the time and remained so for vehicles on occupation duty.

A Panzer IV Ausf J with the 2nd SS *Das Reich* in France. *Das Reich* was upgraded to a full panzer division in Bordeaux early in 1944. SS panzer divisions had a battalion of Mk IVs and a battalion of Panthers, as well as an assault gun detachment. At the beginning of June 1944 *Das Reich* had only forty-five Panzer IVs; another twenty-four were delivered in the middle of the month.

The Tiger I was first blooded in the winter of 1942. It served with the Waffen-SS and the German army's independent heavy panzer battalions on both the Eastern and Western Fronts.

A Tiger I bearing the corps badge of the 1st SS Panzer Corps: crossed keys within a shield above two oakleaves. This reflected Heavy SS Panzer Battalion 101's close links with *Leibstandarte*. The corps in the summer of 1944 consisted of the 1st and 12th SS Panzer Divisions and the 17th SS Panzergrenadier Division.

Tiger 331 of Heavy SS Panzer Battalion 101 pictured in Normandy. This unit, alongside the 12th SS, helped oppose the Allied landings in 1944. Afterwards the unit was re-equipped with Tiger II and supported Kampfgruppe Peiper, drawn from the 1st SS.

The Panther Ausf D went into service in mid-1943. The army's 1st Panzer Division was the initial recipient, followed by *Leibstandarte* and *Das Reich*. The third and final model, the Ausf G, went into production in March 1944.

A StuG III Ausf G belonging to a Waffen-SS assault gun battalion on the Eastern Front. These units were rather weak compared to the panzer battalions and had only twenty StuGs in three companies.

The SdKfz 251 half-track was used to transport SS panzergrenadiers. The smaller vehicle to the left with the radio antenna is a SdKfz 251/3. Each SS panzer division had two panzergrenadier regiments.

Chapter Two

Wiking Trapped at Cherkassy

Collaboration in the Nazi occupied territories was far more widespread than people generally realise. One result of this was that local SS security units were formed that created the basis for many of Himmler's foreign Waffen-SS divisions. Space does not permit any real exploration of this contentious and complex issue in this book but it is worth looking at the experiences of Scandinavia and the Low Countries as they raised an SS panzer division.

A cadre of willing recruits was initially established when the Waffen-SS set up a number of security battalions, principally SS Guard Bn 3 'Nordwest' from Dutch volunteers, SS Guard Bn 6 'Nord' from Norwegians and SS Guard Bn 'Sjaelland' from Danes. The black-clad Allgemeine-SS also established foreign branches in the 'Germanic' (i.e. non-Slavic) occupied countries. This 'Germanic-SS' recruited the most ardent collaborationists in Denmark, Belgium (Flanders), the Netherlands (Holland) and Norway. They likewise provided the volunteers for foreign Waffen-SS units and pro-German security units.

In Denmark the Danish Foreign Minister Erik Scavenius supported the anti-Komintern Treaty and the recruitment of Danish volunteers for the Waffen-SS to fight the Soviet Union. The Schalburg Korpset was also raised as a Danish branch of the Germanic-SS although it never adopted the SS designation. It recruited Danish SS Eastern Front veterans for an internal security role.

In February 1942 Germany appointed Vidkun Quisling 'Minister President' of Norway, although power really rested with the Reichskommissar. Jonas Lie was Quisling's Minister of Justice and Police and leader of the Norwegian Germanic-SS. In Norway an Allgemeine-SS unit was formed, initially known as the *Norges-SS* but later retitled the *Germanske-SS Norge* – presumably to emphasise its Germanic credentials. This was about 1,300 strong and wore black uniforms.

In Holland the Dutch fascists formed the *Nederlandsche-SS*, which was later renamed the *Germansche-SS en Nederland*. These troops also wore black uniforms. The 11,000-strong *Landstorm Nederland* militia also came under the SS. This was later amalgamated with the SS Guard Battalion *Nordwest* to create the so-called 34th SS-Freiwilligen Grenadier Division *Landstorm Nederland*.

The 5th SS Panzer Division *Wiking* was the first and best of the foreign units raised by the Waffen-SS. Gottlob Berger's foreign recruiting drive began to gather momentum in December 1940. The *Germania* Regiment of the SS-VT Division was set aside to form the cadre of a new division recruited from Europeans within the occupied territories. Added to this were two foreign regiments already formed that year, the Scandinavian Standarte *Nordland* using 216 Danish and 294 Norwegian volunteers, and the Standarte *Westland* with 630 Dutch and Flemish recruits. A Finnish battalion, *Nordost*, was added in 1941 but later broken up as replacements. These units eventually became the SS Panzergrenadier Regiment 9 *Germania* and SS Panzergrenadier 10 *Westland*.

The new division, initially known as *Germania*, was placed under General Felix Steiner. He had his work cut out melding his disparate recruits into an effective unit. Initially, discrimination by German officers and instructors proved problematic, forcing Steiner to issue an order calling for humane leadership. To reflect the division's Nordic origins, and to make the volunteers feel more welcome, it was renamed *Wiking*.

Wiking initially took part in the invasion of the Soviet Union as a motorised division. The following year it fought in the Caucasus and was redesignated a panzergrenadier division. In the spring of 1943 the 5th SS was involved in the counter-offensive between the Don and Dneiper. Afterwards the *Nordland* Regiment was detached to create the nucleus of the 11th SS Freiwilligen Panzergrenadier Division of the same name. It was partially replaced by an Estonian battalion. *Wiking* took part in the fighting at Kursk in the summer of 1943 and at the end of the year, with the addition of a tank battalion, *Wiking* became a panzer division.

In early February 1944 the Red Army's 1st and 2nd Ukrainian Fronts linked up near Zvenigorodka, trapping 56,000 troops of the German 11th and 42nd Corps in the Cherkassy or Korsun pocket, around 100 miles southeast of Kiev. Some 35 Soviet divisions surrounded the pocket. The German corps in the pocket commanded six divisions, including *Wiking* and what became Leon Dégrelle's 28th SS Freiwilligen Panzergrenadier Division *Wallonien*.

At the time the latter was only of brigade strength, some 2,000 strong, having been taken over from the army as the Freiwilligen SS-Sturmbrigade *Wallonien* in June 1943. This was attached attached to *Wiking*. Under SS-Obergruppenführer Herbert Otto Gille, who had replaced Felix Steiner in May 1943, the 5th SS, numbering some 11,400 men, had fewer than fifty panzers and self-propelled guns and fewer than fifty pieces of artillery.

The plan was for a two-pronged relief, with 1st Panzer Army's 3rd Panzer Corps driving from the southwest and 8th Army's 47th Panzer Corps striking from the south.

Despite their losses of transport aircraft at Stalingrad, the Luftwaffe was expected to provide an air bridge to the pocket. As far as Hitler was concerned, the highly successful 1942 Demyansk airlift would be repeated. Weather and road conditions were such that the two relief corps had to be resupplied by air as well. In the event, the Red Air Force shot the Luftwaffe out the sky as it struggled to keep the trapped troops resupplied. In addition, 47th Panzer Corps was reduced to just sixty-one panzers and assault guns, and could do little more than conduct local attacks.

Hitler ordered the surrounded corps to stay put while four panzer divisions, including the 1st SS, tried to cut their way through. The 16th and 17th Panzer Divisions of 3rd Panzer Corps attempted to reach the pocket, pushing northward on 4 February. In the meantime Hitler signalled General Stemmermann in the Cherkassy pocket, saying: 'You can rely on me like you would on a wall of stone. You will be freed from the ring. For the time being hold on.' But Stemmermann had no intention of holding on; he rejected an offer to surrender on the 9th and Zhukov signalled Stalin:

> According to information received from PoWs, during battles in encirclement enemy troops have sustained heavy losses and their officers and men are now in a state of confusion bordering on panic.
>
> According to intelligence reports surrounded enemy forces have concentrated [the] bulk of their troops in [the] Steblev-Korsun-Shevchenkovsky area. The enemy is apparently preparing for [a] last attempt to break out towards Panzer group advancing on Malaya Boyarka.

The German counter-attack quickly bogged down, so the 1st SS and 1st Panzer Divisions struck southward, getting as far as Lysyanka, just 5 miles from the pocket. Unfortunately for the trapped men, 3rd Panzer Corps just did not have the strength to make the final push. By 10 February the pocket was just 6 miles by 7. Tanks of SS Panzer Regiment 1 cut through four Russian divisions, but the depleted 1st SS was left with just three panzers and four assault guns.

Hitler was normally averse to surrendering ground but now agreed to a breakout attempt. The order was finally transmitted to Stemmermann on 15 February informing him that he could expect no further help:

> Capabilities of III Panzer Corps reduced by weather and supply difficulties. Task Force Stemmermann must accomplish break-through on its own to line Dzhurzhentsy-Hill 239 where it will link up with 3rd Panzer Corps. The breakout force will be under the command of General Lieb [42nd Corps] and comprise all units still capable of attack.

The 5th SS Panzer Division led the desperate attempt to break out on the 16th, only to run into the 4th Guards and 27th Armies. *Wiking* punched westwards through a snowstorm, while the men of the *Wallonien* brigade covered the retreat and held open the corridor. This they did with distinction, with only 632 of their number surviving unscathed. *Wiking* fought its way to the Gniloi-Tilkitsch river but could find no bridges or fords, so in desperation human chains were formed to help non-swimmers cross.

In the bitter fighting the Germans lost 20,000 killed and 8,000 captured. The Soviets claimed that the battle for Korsun-Shevchenkovsky cost the Germans a total of 55,000 killed or wounded and 18,200 captured. The Germans maintained that 30,000 men managed to escape the pocket, largely thanks to the actions of *Wiking*.

In crossing the Gniloi-Tilkitsch river the 5th SS lost all of its armour and most of its heavy equipment. Although the 11th and 42nd Corps escaped, they were severely depleted and were pulled from the line. This greatly impacted on the defensive effort of Army Group South in fending off attacks in the Uman area.

In late March 1944 some 200,000 troops of the 1st Panzer Army, including weak battle groups from *Leibstandarte* with 3rd Panzer Corps and *Das Reich* with 59th Army Corps, were caught in the Kamenets-Podolskiy area. By mid-March the 1st SS had fewer than 1,250 men and the 2nd SS around 2,500. The bulk of the latter had been sent to East Prussia at the end of 1943 to reorganise with a full complement of Panther and Tiger tanks. In early February elements of the division had started arriving at their new training ground in Bordeaux.

The forces trapped at Kamenets-Podolskiy could not escape the enveloping Red Army, so the newly operational 9th and 10th SS Panzer Divisions *Hohenstaufen* and *Frundsberg* were sent to their rescue. Although the weather was appalling, they managed to break through to 1st Panzer Army as it fought its way westward through freezing fog. Kampfgruppe Lammerding (named after its commander, Oberführer Heinz Lammerding) from the 2nd SS formed the rearguard while the other German units escaped to safety.

Most of the troops of 1st Panzer Army were successfully rescued but they lost all their heavy equipment and only forty-five armoured vehicles were saved. The LSSAH battle group was rescued but suffered heavy losses. The remains of the division were then sent to Belgium for rest and refitting in 15th Army's area of responsibility. Kampfgruppe Lammerding was also sent to Bordeaux, though the small Kampfgruppe Weidinger remained on the Eastern Front. It was involved in the fighting retreat through Proskurov and Tarnopol.

It was at Cherkassy that the last of Hitler's offensive strength in Ukraine was lost, creating the conditions for the victorious Red Army advances in the summer and autumn of 1944. SS-Obergruppenführer Gille reported to Hitler that *Wiking* had ceased to exist as a combat division. The 5th SS survivors were withdrawn to Breslau to refit, though a 4,000-strong battle group remained on the Eastern Front. The division next saw action in July 1944 when it was sent to help bolster the Vistula Front in Poland.

Léon Degrelle gained the Knight's Cross of the Iron Cross for his leadership of his Sturmbrigade during the breakout. On returning home the survivors held a celebration in Brussels on 1 April 1944, with 'Sepp' Dietrich as the guest of honour. Cherkassy cost SS-Untersturmführer Jaques Leroy his right eye and right arm but he refused to be invalided out of the brigade. The bravery of Degrelle's Walloons convinced the SS of their worth and he was given permission to form a panzergrenadier division, though it never reached full strength.

Leibstandarte and its supporting Tigers struggling through the mud on the Eastern Front at the end of 1943. The winter of 1943/44 proved a particularly challenging time for the Waffen-SS.

Members of the 5th SS Panzer Division *Wiking*'s tank destroyer detachment equipped with the Marder II. Judging by the vehicle's very light colour, it has a whitewash over the *dunkel gelb* (deep sand yellow) base coat. The division contained Danes, Dutch, Flemings, Germans, Walloons, Norwegians and Finns. It first saw action as part of Operation Barbarossa in 1941. The man on the right is SS-Hauptsturmführer Oeck, the tank destroyer commander. His NCO has a peaked field cap in camouflage pattern. The division's reputation was forged at Cherkassy.

Panzer IVs and men of the 5th SS caught in a swirling blizzard. In early February 1944 the Red Army trapped 56,000 German troops from units including *Wiking* and the SS-Sturmbrigade *Wallonien*, drawn from volunteers from Scandinavia and the Low Countries.

Tanks and half-tracks massing for the attempt to cut through to the trapped 11th and 42nd Corps at Cherkassy. Success rested on the four panzer divisions of the 3rd Panzer Corps, which included the weak 1st SS.

Whitewashed Panzer IVs on the Russian steppe preparing for the rescue operation.

Well camouflaged Tiger Is and supporting infantry. The Cherkassy relief force also included Heavy Panzer Regiment Bäke with Panther and Tiger tanks. The regiment was subsequently trapped in the Kamenets-Podolskiy pocket, along with the whole of the 1st Panzer Army.

Wrapped up against the cold, this grenadier has a warm drink before going into action.

Softening up the enemy. A Hummel on the Eastern Front in early 1944; these were used to equip elements of the SS panzer divisions' artillery regiments.

Towed German artillery laying down covering fire.

Panzer IVs loaded with infantry. When the relief force was held up, the 5th SS was ordered to lead the breakout.

German troops in camouflaged parkas trying to escape Soviet encirclement. Broken down motor vehicles have been pushed off the road to allow the horse-drawn wagons to pass.

German equipment abandoned in the Cherkassy pocket. During the breakout the 5th SS lost all its heavy equipment, including its remaining panzers.

Sheltering in his foxhole on 21 March 1944, a German solder glances at a knocked out T-34 tank. The Germans were again encircled, this time in the Kamenets-Podolskiy pocket. This contained some 200,000 men, including battlegroups from the 1st and 2nd SS Panzer Divisions.

Soviet infantry hurry past a burning Panzer IV in Tarnopol to the northwest of the Kamenets-Podolskiy pocket.

Panthers being unloaded from trains in March 1944. Note the damaged StuG on the left. To save the Kamenets-Podolskiy pocket required the intervention of the Panthers of the newly operational 9th and 10th SS Panzer Divisions *Hohenstaufen* and *Frundsberg*.

Hohenstaufen Division Hummel self-propelled guns and Hummel ammunition carriers on their way to the front. They are painted in a dark base colour, presumably panzer grey, with sprayed patches of lighter camouflage either *oliv grun* (olive green) or *rotbraun* (reddish brown). This clearly made them stand out against the winter landscape.

Despatch riders wait for a Tiger I to pass. The tank is finished in *dunkel gelb* overpainted with a rough whitewash camouflage.

Léon Degrelle awarding medals to rather sombre survivors of his Freiwilligen SS-Sturmbrigade *Wallonien* in Charleroi, Belgium. These men had escaped Cherkassy. A celebratory dinner was held in Brussels on 1 April 1944, with 'Sepp' Dietrich, just visible second from the left, as guest of honour. The brigade fought with the 5th SS, suffering 1,368 killed and wounded from a total of 2,000 men.

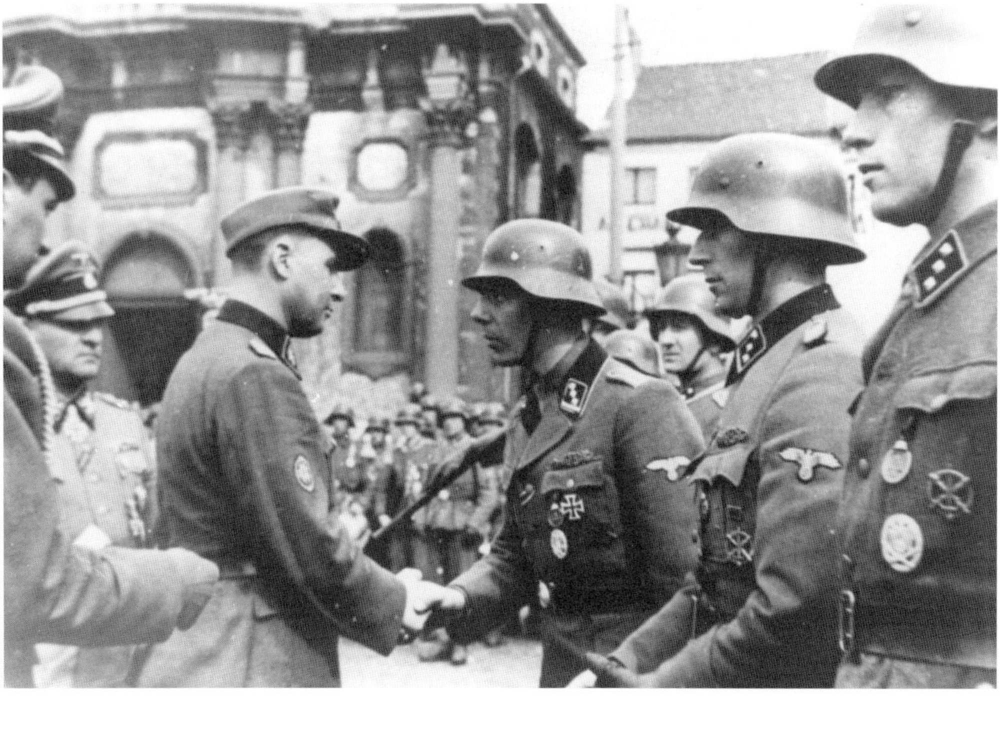

Chapter Three

Hitlerjugend at Ardenne Abbey

On D-Day, 6 June 1944, Hitler dithered, hoping that his infantry would hold the invasion. After midday he passed control of the 12th SS Panzer Division *Hitlerjugend* over to General Dollman's 7th Army. SS-Standartenführer Kurt Meyer, commander of SS Panzergrenadier Regiment 25, came under air attack that day, as he graphically relates: 'A chain of Spitfires attacks the last section of the 15th Company. Missiles and cannon reap a devilish harvest.' The divisional reconnaissance battalion, under SS-Sturmbannführer and Ritterkreuzträger Gerd Bremer, was among the first units to reach the front on the 7th. Upon arrival, it manoeuvred through 8 miles of no man's land to the division's far left flank to establish a security line. The battalion beat off numerous heavy attacks between 7 and 11 June, during which Bremer's command vehicle was knocked out and he was wounded by shrapnel. Although twice wounded, he nevertheless remained with his unit until the situation was secure.

Shortly after Kurt Meyer arrived, he galvanised the situation, proposing a counter-attack on the left flank of 21st Panzer. He established his HQ at Ardenne Abbey, outside Caen. His SS Panzergrenadier Regiment 25, part of Kampfgruppe Meyer/Wünsche, went into action against the Canadians north of the city on 7 June, supported by fifty Panzer IVs of 2nd Battalion SS Panzer Regiment 12 commanded by Sturmbannführer Prinz. The counter-attack was timed for 1600, but four Panzer IVs of 5th Company under Untersturmführer Porsh ran into Sherman tanks along the Franqueville-Authie road. Three of the panzers were knocked out and it became impossible to wait. Wünsche gave the order and the 5th and 6th Companies advanced left of Ardenne Abbey, with the 6th Company claiming ten enemy tanks for the loss of five Panzer IVs.

SS-Sturmann Hans Fenn was almost killed in this battle:

> Ours, the fifth panzer, took a direct hit between the side of the hull and the turret . . . The shell ripped a leg off my commander, Oberscharführer Esser. As I heard later, he managed to get out of the turret. The incendiary shell immediately set fire to all parts of the panzer. I lost consciousness. . . .

Somehow, I managed, without being fully conscious, to crawl over the hatch of the loader.

The attack was broken up by Canadian artillery, naval gunfire and air strikes, followed by a counter-attack by the Sherbrooke Fusiliers. That evening the Kampfgruppe of panzergrenadiers and panzers held defensive positions stretching from the railway line between Caen and Luc sur Mer to Rue Nationale 13 from Caen to Bayeux. Although the Canadians had pushed through the Carpiquet airfield, the 12th SS had stopped them in their tracks, destroying a total of twenty-seven tanks for the loss of fourteen Panzer IVs. Over the next few days the Canadian 3rd Infantry Division, striking from the Caen–Bayeux railway near Bretteville, fought the 12th SS.

The 12th SS found Carpiquet airfield deserted by the Luftwaffe and unoccupied by the Canadians. They now turned on the Canadian 7th Brigade, also part of the Canadian 3rd Division. Around 2200 SS Panzergrenadier Regiment 25, supported by Panthers, struck towards Bretteville from three directions. The attack from the south resulted in the platoon commander's tank being immobilised in the town and surrounded. The attack from the southwest was ordered to rescue him, but the lead tank was knocked out and driven off. In the attack from the west three Panthers were hit simultaneously by concealed Canadian anti-tank guns; two managed to withdraw, but the other burned like a torch, although its crew managed to escape. The following morning the attack was broken off.

On 9 June Panthers of 3rd Company, SS Panzer Regiment 12, under SS-Obersturmführer Rudolf von Ribbentrop, having missed the attack on Bretteville, moved on Norrey with the Caen–Cherbourg railway embankment protecting its right flank. Ribbentrop had been wounded so Hauptmann Lüdman led the twelve Panthers. However, once they advanced beyond the cover of the railway bank, well concealed anti-tank guns knocked out seven Panthers and the advance was halted. Crew losses were also heavy, with eighteen of the thirty-five men involved killed.

The 3rd Company then moved to Fontenay-les-Pesnel to the west, but with all its tanks suffering mechanical problems withdrew to Harcourt. Two days later the division's tanks claimed thirty-seven Shermans for the loss of three panzers in the fighting south of Le Mesnil.

The stark reality of war soon came home to Emil Werner, serving with Meyer's SS Panzergrenadier Regiment 25:

Until Cambes everything went well. So far as we were concerned, the village looked fine. But on the outskirts we came under infantry fire and then all hell broke loose. We stormed a church where snipers had taken up positions.

Here I saw the first dead man from our kompanie; it was Grenadier Ruehl from the headquarters platoon. I turned his body over myself – he'd been shot through the head.

On the 11th the Canadian 6th Armoured Regiment lost thirty-seven of its seventy-six tanks in the fighting around Le Mensil-Patry. By now the 12th SS had lost about 25 per cent of its manpower, 20 per cent of its tanks and 10 per cent of its guns. In total, about sixty Panzer IV and V tanks remained serviceable. Fritz Witt was killed at Venoix on the morning of the 14th when his HQ was caught in an Allied naval bombardment and shrapnel struck him in the face. Following his death, Kurt 'Panzer' Meyer took command of the division.

It seemed that the British Operation Epsom, designed to punch west of Caen on 25 June, could not fail, but directly in its path lay the 12th SS, holding the line from Fontenay-le-Pesnil through St Marvieu and Cheux eastwards to Carpiquet airfield. The British 30th Corps was to jump off first, followed by 8th Corps the next day. The latter had 60,000 men, 600 tanks, 300 guns and the support of another 400 guns from the flanking 30th Corps, plus naval and air support. It fell to SS Panzer Regiment 12 and SS Panzergrenadier Regiment 25 to resist 8th Corps, while just to the west of Caen SS Panzergrenadier Regiment 26 was facing the Canadian 3rd Division.

The plan was for the British 8th Corps to break through between 47th Panzer Corps and 1st SS Panzer Corps, force a bridgehead over the Odon river and take the strategic height of Hill 112. For the British it was a race against time as the 2nd SS Panzer Corps and 2nd SS Panzer Division were heading for the sector, so even if the attack pierced the in-depth defences of the 12th SS, the intervention of German armoured reinforcements could kill Epsom. On 25 June 30th Corps conducted Operation Dauntless, a subsidiary attack to secure 8th Corps' western flank before the main offensive carried out by the 49th (West Riding) Infantry Division supported by the 8th Armoured Brigade. The 49th also conducted Operation Martlet, intended to capture Fontenay-le-Pesnil.

Second Lieutenant Stuart Hills of the Nottinghamshire Sherwood Rangers Yeomanry, 8th Armoured Brigade, remembered the stiff reception from the 12th SS:

> The fighting in Fontenay was fierce and confused, with enemy tanks of 12th SS Panzer dug in defensively east of the town, and we did not have enough infantry to take the village. At about four o'clock in the afternoon the attack had clearly run out of steam, infantry losses had been heavy and we withdrew to the heights of Point 102 above Fontenay to replenish our stocks of ammunition, refuel and have something to eat.

The attack, though, was renewed and Fontenay was duly captured and the road to Caen cut. A Squadron moved forward to attack Rauray but, as Stuart Hills relates, it was in for a nasty surprise:

> As they cleared Fontenay, they were suddenly confronted by an enormous tank coming round the bend in front. It was hard to know who was more surprised, but John [Semken, the squadron leader] shrieked, 'Fire, it's a Hun,' and they loosed off about ten rounds into the smoke. As this cleared away, it was observed that the crew were baling out as small flames came from inside the tank. It was a Tiger of 12th SS Panzer, the first Tiger to be captured in Normandy, and [it] made an impressive sight at close quarters as both its size and the thickness of its armour became apparent.

Semken's force included a number of Sherman Fireflys armed with the powerful 17-pounder anti-tank gun and by the end of the day they had accounted for thirteen Panzer IVs, a Tiger and a Panther tank.

Between Tessel Wood and Rauray ten Tiger tanks were dug in and SS Panzer Regiment 26 repulsed the British attack through Le Manoir from Tessel towards Rauray and established positions near Le Haut du Bosc facing towards Cheux. Assembling across the line Fontenay-Tessel-Bretteville to attack towards Juvigny, the Heavy Tank Company's actions left SS Panzergrenadier Regiment 26, which lay directly in the path of the British attack, unsupported. The latter was thrown into a counter-attack at 0500 on the 26th.

Hubert Meyer, Operations Staff Officer of the 12th SS, was expecting an armoured attack and tried to get the order rescinded, but 1st SS Panzer Corps would not comply. The results were predictable:

> At 0700 on 26 June, this great British attack of about 500–600 tanks on a breadth of about 3 miles rolled over the Pioneers and the Panzergrenadiers. Eventually it came to a halt only because our artillery fire separated the enemy infantry from their tanks. . . . As late as 28 June our operators picked up radio messages from British tanks attacking the remnants of 3rd Pioneer Company, which still held several strongpoints in the old front line between St. Mauvieu and Fontenay. We tried to convince 1st SS Panzer Corps that a well planned counter-attack by tank units from the southwest might restore the original front, or at least, relieve the surrounded units, but fresh forces were not available.

The 15th (Scottish) Division, with the 11th Armoured Division and the 31st Tank Brigade, also broke through the 12th SS's defences. Likewise the 43rd (Wessex)

Division, supported by the 4th Armoured Brigade, reached Mouen. On the 27th the 15th (Scottish) Division captured a bridge over the Odon and the 11th Armoured Division moved to take Hill 112.

The following day British tanks and air attacks drove the enemy from the hill. The British 20th Armoured Brigade withdrew from Hill 112 on the night of 29/30 June, not because of dogged resistance by 12th SS but in response to the arrival of 2nd SS Panzer Corps with the 9th and 10th SS Panzer Divisions, which came into the line between 47th Panzer Corps and 1st SS Panzer Corps. The Germans had succeeded in containing Epsom but at a cost of more than 2,600 casualties sustained by the 12th SS. Epsom cost the British 8th Corps 4,020 casualties, while the 11th Armoured Division alone lost a hundred tanks and suffered 1,000 casualties during 26–29 June.

On 6 July panzergrenadiers of the 12th SS deployed to the northern suburbs of Caen. Within two days they, along with a regiment from the 16th Luftwaffe Field Division, were ejected by Montgomery's Operation Charnwood, a frontal assault on the city that commenced on the 7th. The Canadians sought to exploit their gains at Carpiquet, striking Caen from the west. To the east the 3rd Infantry was to secure Lebisey and Herouville, their original D-Day objectives. The bombing, while impeding the progress of the attackers, did not completely neutralise the defenders and 7.5cm and 8.8cm anti-tank guns met the tanks. At La Bijude the 12th SS troops were well entrenched and it took two attempts before the village was firmly in the 59th Division's hands. The advancing Allies were then brought to a halt before Malan.

The British 3rd Division reached Lebisey and Herouville within an hour and brushed aside the 16th Luftwaffe Field Division only to find Caen an impassable sea of craters and rubble. In the meantime the 1st SS tried to mass its armour for a counter-attack, but air strikes and naval gunfire drove back the thirty-five panzers, which suffered some losses.

At the village of Buron, northwest of Caen, elements of the 3rd Battalion, SS Panzergrenadier Regiment 25, were surrounded and on the verge of being overrun by Canadian tanks. Kurt Meyer and General Eberbach, Panzergruppe West's commander, were at the Ardenne Abbey. Meyer recalled the dramatically unfolding events:

> All available tanks were sent towards Buron. The attack failed to get through. From the [Ardenne] monastery church tower I watched the tank fight as it surged back and forth. Both sides suffered heavy losses. Then, suddenly, enemy tanks appeared from Authi [to the north], heading straight for Ardenne.

The fifteen Panthers of von Ribbentrop's tank company now deployed against this mass of enemy tanks and they shot up the enemy armour, halting its advance.

The last enemy tank was destroyed only 100 metres west of Ardenne but von Ribbentrop had saved the command post. His initial instructions had been to relieve the panzergrenadiers and clear the Canadians from Buron, but he was distracted by the Canadian tanks to the left of the village and had to send a platoon of Panthers to deal with them. Reaching Buron, von Ribbentrop's Panthers knocked out several Canadian tanks.

SS-Unterscharführer Freiberg, serving with von Ribbentrop, was in one of the three knocked-out Panthers:

> We crossed the open field to the wall around the village of Buron at high speed. As we moved past an opening in the wall, there were suddenly two explosions. Sepp Trattnick's tank and another tank burst into flames. We immediately opened fire with both machine guns on the opening in the wall. I saw some movement there and then a flash from the muzzle of an anti-tank gun. The round struck our gun mantlet and the solid projectile ended up in the fighting compartment. Our sight was smashed, and the gunner was wounded in the face. I received several fragments in my left arm.

Although the troops of the 12th SS could not retain Caen, they had, along with Panzer Lehr, denied it to the Allies for just over a month. By the 9th the 12th SS had lost fifty-one Panzer IVs and thirty-two Panthers. Three days later the men received a welcome respite from the bloodletting when they were relieved by an infantry division and sent to Potigny, 20 miles north of Falaise, to recuperate. After the liberation of Ardenne Abbey it was later discovered that the 12th SS had slaughtered twenty Canadian prisoners in the grounds in early June 1944. After the war Kurt Meyer was put on trial for this war crime.

By the end of 10 August Meyer had just thirty-five panzers facing some 700 enemy tanks. However, in the area defended by the 12th SS alone, more than a hundred Allied tanks were destroyed in the fierce close combat. By now the American breakout from Avranches was well under way and the US 1st and 3rd Armies were charging westward. Although the Canadians reached Falaise on 16 August, the 12th SS held out in the town for a further two days. By now the battle for Normandy was all but over.

Between 6 June and 22 August Hitler's fanatical and resolutely fearless teenage Nazis lost around 8,000 men killed in action, wounded and missing. This must have seemed a death-blow from which no unit could hope to recover. Nonetheless, most of the division's combat arms and rear services were not encircled at Falaise. In addition, many of the missing who evaded capture made their way back to the unit. It would soon rise from the ashes of Normandy ready to fight again.

Very young Hitler Youth being introduced to panzergrenadiers of the 12th SS Panzer Division *Hitlerjugend* in Belgium in 1944. At least three of the SS panzer divisions recruited Nazi-indoctrinated teenagers.

A young panzergrenadier of 12th SS Panzer Division *Hitlerjugend*. The recruits for this division were drawn from 17-year-old members of the Hitler Youth in 1943. Kurt Meyer's SS Panzergrenadier Regiment 25 went into action against the Canadians in Normandy on 7 June 1944.

Two more SS panzergrenadiers in Waffen-SS smocks and with fabric helmet covers. *Hitlerjugend* arrived in Normandy with about 17,000 men, which included two panzergrenadier regiments.

Hitlerjugend Panzer IVs in France in 1944. SS Panzer Regiment 12 under SS-Obersturmbannführer Max Wünche had an authorised strength of around a hundred Panzer IVs and eighty Panthers. These were massed in the Ardenne Abbey area.

A Waffen-SS Panther passing through Paris to the front. The SS panzertruppen are wearing the one-piece non-reversible camouflage coverall.

A Wespe 105mm self-propelled gun belonging to SS Panzer Artillery Regiment 12 from the 12th SS Panzer Division *Hitlerjugend*. An SS panzer artillery regiment comprised twelve batteries in four battalions. One battery in each battalion was equipped with self-propelled guns, whilst the rest were towed weapons. In the summer of 1944 *Hitlerjugend* had twelve Wespe and six Hummel self-propelled guns.

Panzertruppen and panzergrenadiers from the 12th SS in the Ardenne Abbey area in early June 1944.

Hitlerjugend commander Fritz Witt (*centre*) in conference with Max Wünsche, commander of the 12th SS Panzer Regiment (*right*), and Kurt Meyer, commander of the 25th SS Panzergrenadier Regiment (*left*). Witt was killed on 14 June.

Wrecked half-tracks destroyed during the bitter fighting in Normandy.

A Sherman tank knocked out by the 12th SS during early July.

A knocked-out 12th SS Panther in Fontenay-le-Pensel, west of Caen. It was destroyed during Operation Martel on 25 June 1944. In the foreground is a Waffen-SS gunner and his 75mm anti-tank gun.

Some twenty Tigers of Heavy SS Panzer Battalion 101 fought with the 12th SS as part of Kampfgruppe Wünsche. Max Wünsche was the commander of the 12th SS Panzer Regiment.

12th SS Panzer IV Ausf H. After divisional commander Fritz Witt was killed, Kurt Meyer took charge. His tanks gave the Canadians a tough time at Buron.

A Jagdpanzer IV lost in France. On 19 July 1944 SS Panzerjäger Abteilung 12 joined *Hitlerjugend* with a company of Jagdpanzer IV. On 26 April the division had ten such tank destroyers and another eleven were sent on 22 June.

Chapter Four

Hohenstaufen's Normandy Hills

As part of Paul Hausser's 2nd SS Panzer Corps, the 9th SS *Hohenstaufen* moved to Normandy with its sister division, the 10th SS *Frundsberg*. It took them longer to reach Caen from the French border than it had taken to make the journey from Poland to France. All German reinforcements from the east were delayed by virtue of having to pass through the Chartres gap between the Seine and the Loire, which was vulnerable to air attack and French sabotage.

The 9th SS *Hohenstaufen* division reached the French border on 16 June, but it was another four days before the lead elements were unloaded from their railway carriages between Paris and Nancy. It then assembled south of Aunay-sur-Odon with a total of 18,000 men, 170 panzers, 21 self-propelled guns, 287 armoured half-tracks, 16 armoured cars and 3,670 trucks. Initially the division was deployed south of a line that ran from Falaise to Condé-sur-Noireau, but it then moved north between Caen and Villers-Bocage on a line between Tournay-sur-Odon and Neuilly-le-Malherbe.

At a critical moment before their counter-attack the Germans were forced to conduct one of their habitual command reshuffles. 'Willi' Bittrich suddenly found himself commanding 2nd SS Panzer Corps after Hausser succeeded General Dollmann as commander of 7th Army when he dropped dead on 28 June of a suspected heart attack (although General Max Pemsel, his Chief of the General Staff, suspected he may have poisoned himself).

Hausser, with 2nd SS Panzer Corps, organised the counter-attack using the 9th SS. This was scheduled to begin at 0700 on 29 June with the 9th SS on the left of the Odon, but attacks by the RAF delayed the preparations until 1430. In addition, in a stroke of bad luck for the Germans, an officer from the 9th SS, with the plans for the coming attack, was out early reconnoitring the routes to Cheux when he was captured. The first group of SS troops captured Grainville-sur-Odon and the second group also reached Cheux, but everywhere else the British and Canadians held fast. Several flame-throwing tanks also assisted with the assault on Le Valtru, but although the panzers overran the British infantry, the latter held firm.

During the fighting against the Epsom salient, the 9th SS suffered 1,145 casualties and lost sixteen Panzer IVs, six Panthers and ten assault guns. Over the next few days the division's assault guns accounted for forty-nine enemy tanks, while its Panzer IVs and Panthers claimed another thirteen.

In July SS-Brigadeführer Sylvester Stadler took command of the 9th SS, having previously commanded Panzergrenadier Regiment *Der Führer* of the 2nd SS Panzer Division. It was units of this regiment, under SS-Sturmbannführer Otto Diekmann, that had conducted the massacre at Oradour-sur-Glane during the division's march northward to Normandy. Stadler was an experienced Eastern Front veteran, having gained the Knight's Cross for his part in the capture of Kharkov in 1943. He had then gained the Oak Leaves for the award after his involvement in the massive battle of Kursk. Thomas Müller, who had been acting commander of the 9th SS, subsequently assumed command of the 17th SS Panzergrenadier Division for a brief period in September, after SS-Oberführer Eduard Deisenhofer was wounded.

Stadler quickly found his division being thrown into action and recalled the details of the battle:

> Within one hour after the division had been taken over, orders for a counter-attack on Maltot, Etenrille and on Baron by way of Hill 112 were received from the Corps by telephone, and a short time later confirmed in writing. So the attack on Baron was to be launched at 2000 and that on Eterville at 1200. Although the time was very short, the execution of this task was still possible thanks to the fact that the SS Panzergrenadier Regiment 20 was not too far away and that a tank battalion, together with the artillery, could support the operation from the positions they were in at the time.

Things did not run smoothly as the Allies did all they could to impede the massing of the 9th SS, and in addition its position was compromised by the loss of Hill 112. The latter was to become the scene of heavy casualties for both sides. Stadler discovered flexibility was an increasing prerequisite of such operations:

> Concentration of the division was greatly impeded and delayed by serious traffic jams on roads, harassing fire from the enemy artillery directed on villages along the routes of advance and on road junctions, as well as by the strong enemy air activity. In addition to that, the enemy managed at about 1800 to capture Height 112, which dominated the entire Corps sector. Thereupon the mission assigned to the division was altered by the Corps, to the effect that only Height 112, and later Eterville, had to be recaptured.

The British quickly contested the 9th SS's successes at Eterville and Hill 112 on the 4th. The panzers managed to knock out a number of British tanks, for little loss, but the panzergrenadiers suffered from the enemy's artillery. Stadler recalled, perhaps with some pride:

> In the course of the forenoon the enemy, in turn, resumed his attacks and managed to take Eterville once again, whereas his attacks on Height 112 were repelled with considerable losses. A counter-attack launched immediately on Eterville succeeded and, by noon, the village was again in our hands. An extremely heavy and fluctuating battle ensued afterwards for the ruins of Eterville, which place changed hands repeatedly until, finally, it was firmly in our possession late in the evening of 4 July 1944. . . . Nevertheless, the panzer Abteilung operating near Eterville managed to destroy twelve to fourteen enemy vehicles, whereas they lost only two tanks. Thus, it could be figured out that the enemy losses were at least as high as ours.

During the night of 4/5 July the division was relieved on the eastern sector by elements of the 12th SS and on the western sector by the 10th SS. The British renewed their attacks on 6 July, this time along the road running from Caen to Noyers. To help the 277th Infantry Division recapture Noyers the 9th SS despatched its armoured reconnaissance battalion. The latter successfully retook the town and remained there in support of the 277th.

The panzers' regimental HQ was established on 12 July at Bully, about 2.5 miles east of Point 112, between Caen and Evrecy. When the British attacked between Gavrus and Noyers-Bocage four days later, the division's tanks were undergoing maintenance. However, the 277th was ordered to counter-attack, supported by the 9th SS. About twenty panzers were mustered to the right of Point 113 north of Evrecy, but the British put down smoke and they were forced to withdraw. While Point 113 remained unoccupied, the panzers took Bougy and reached Gavrus, moving up the Orne valley. During the various engagements they knocked out a total of forty tanks, including eighteen around Bougy and eight at Point 113 for the loss of just five panzers.

Sylvester Stadler recalled the battle:

> A serious crisis occurred only once on the occasion of a concentrated attack carried out by British armoured troops with some forty to fifty tanks late in the evening of 16 or 17 July 1944, on Height 113. All day, the enemy had pounded the hill with undiminished intensity and covered it with a

smokescreen. Sometimes, the smoke was so dense that the majority of the troops felt sick and therefore believed that the enemy was using gas.

Stadler remembered the sudden British armed assault which came late in the day and threatened to overwhelm his men. The men of the 9th SS, though, were quick witted and swiftly turned the tables on their attackers, as their commander noted:

> Our own tanks, a battalion of about fifteen to twenty tanks, were located on the rear slope of the hill and noticed the enemy only at the very last moment, either on account of the dense smoke, or perhaps owing to the swift and surprising advance of his forces. During the ensuing tank battle, fifteen enemy tanks were destroyed with no losses at all on our side.

By the 17th the exhausted division could muster just thirty-three panzers and fifteen assault guns, while the infantry amounted to little more than a regiment. The 9th SS was called back from the left flank of the 10th SS at the height of the Goodwood battle and positioned in the Orne valley, guarding the southern suburbs of Caen. Over the next few days the 9th SS helped the 1st SS defeat Montgomery's Goodwood armoured offensive. Notably, on 18 July the division captured sixty-seven tanks, fifty-six of which were destroyed, the rest still running.

The 10th SS and the 272nd Infantry Division were instructed to retake St Martin, St André and May-sur-Orne east of the river and south of Caen on the 22nd with support from the 9th SS. However, the Panthers of the 9th SS were still engaged around Bougy and could only be freed up slowly. Some were assigned to two companies of the 10th SS, while the rest were to attack south of May. Few of the Panthers materialised, except for those directed to take the high ground northeast of May.

On 30 July Montgomery launched Operation Bluecoat southwards towards Vire and Mount Pinçon. By the 31st the 9th SS had lost most of its armour. It remained southwest of Caen until early August, when it moved northeast of Vire. British tanks got to within 5 miles of the town, the very heart of 7th Army's resistance against the Americans. Preferring to counter-attack against the Americans, who were considered inferior fighters, the Germans first had to secure Mont Pinçon against the British to control the network of roads westwards.

The division was relieved by the 1st SS on 1 August and that night a Kampfgruppe under Otto Meyer, including seventeen panzers and assault guns, moved west to take up positions on a line from Arclais to Montchauvet and Montchamp, to the west of Mont Pinçon and between Villers-Bocage and Vire. RAF Typhoons located the SS tank columns in the afternoon of the 2nd and launched

923 sorties, destroying thirteen tanks and seventy-six trucks and holding up the deployment of the German panzers for most of the day. They then held the 15th (Scottish) Division with dug-in tanks, 88mm guns and Nebelwerfer rocket launchers. Those troops at Montchauvet were embroiled in heavy fighting around Point 170 and although surrounded managed to escape.

On 4 August the 9th SS attempted to cut off the British breakthrough at Chênedollé, knocking out thirty-nine Allied tanks in the process. Otto Meyer, near Estry with thirty-two panzers and assault guns, had to block the road northwest of Chênedollé and went over to the defensive. On 11–12 August the division claimed another twenty-two enemy tanks in the unrelenting fighting before escaping Normandy.

Confident *Hitlerjugend* panzertruppen (also identified as *Hohenstaufen*) in France. They are wearing black leather U-boat clothing, comprising jackets and trousers, believed to be specific to this unit. At the beginning of June the 9th SS Panzer Division *Hohenstaufen* had forty-five Panzer IVs, thirty-four Panthers and forty StuG IIIs.

This grimy *Hitlerjugend* panzergrenadier barely looks 18. He is armed with an MG42 fitted with a drum magazine (though is also carrying a spare ammunition belt). This weapon with attached bipod weighed just over 25lb, and was capable of firing 1,550 rounds per minute.

Das Reich SdKfz 251 caught on the road in Normandy. *Hohenstaufen* arrived in Normandy with almost 300 of these vehicles.

A Tiger of the 1st SS Panzer Corps in France in 1944. Schwere SS Panzer Abteilung 102 fought with the 2nd SS Panzer Corps in Normandy. Tigers provided the Waffen-SS with added punch in France and were greatly feared by Allied tankers.

The 2nd SS Panzer Corps, comprising the 9th SS and 10th SS *Frundsberg* Panzer Divisions, counter-attacked the Allies' Normandy bridgehead on 29 June 1944. *Hohenstaufen* suffered 1,150 casualties, including this Waffen-SS panzergrenadier who was part of an MG42 team.

This is what greeted the Waffen-SS panzer divisions as they deployed to Normandy. Allied bombers targeted the train yards and main roads to impede movement of the panzers. Such attacks by the RAF delayed preparations for *Hohenstaufen's* counter-attack on 29 June 1944.

Waffen-SS anti-tank gunners manning a PaK40 anti-tank gun. This weapon, along with the PaK38, was the standard towed anti-tank gun deployed in Normandy with both the Waffen-SS and the army.

Destroyed German equipment. The fighting for Hill 112 was brutal, and *Hohenstaufen's* positions were compromised once the Allies had captured it.

Captured teenage Waffen-SS in the distinctive four-pocket camouflage M1944 field tunic and matching trousers. Although it was forbidden to wear insignia on camouflage clothing, they have arm-eagles. The young man on the right is also wearing a Waffen-SS smock. They have been stripped of their personal gear as none is wearing webbing or helmets.

An abandoned SS Hummel self-propelled gun being examined by US troops.

Bloody carnage wrought by Allied fighter-bombers on German horse-drawn transport in the confines of the Bocage. Normandy became plagued by the stench of rotting horseflesh.

Waffen-SS Panthers took a battering in Normandy. This captured Ausf G was used as target practice to gauge the penetration rates of Allied anti-tank weapons of various calibre. The gun mantlet is particularly damaged, as is the glacis plate on the left, which has been fractured.

Passing GIs look on with interest at a decapitated Panther in France. Both the 1st and 2nd SS Panzer Corps escaped Normandy and the Falaise pocket relatively unscathed and lived to fight another day.

Chapter Five

Wiking's Warsaw Triumph

Following Stalin's hugely successful summer offensive in 1944, Field Marshal Model turned to the Waffen-SS for assistance in stabilising the shattered front north of Warsaw. While the 1st SS *Leibstandarte Adolf Hitler* and 2nd SS *Das Reich* Panzer Divisions had been shipped west to re-equip after their mauling in the Kamenets-Podolskiy pocket, the 3rd SS *Totenkopf* and 5th SS *Wiking* Panzer Divisions remained in Romania and Poland, re-arming.

Although the 5th SS may have been the first and best of the foreign Waffen-SS divisions in terms of combat performance, its behaviour left much to be desired. *Wiking*, like so many of its SS counterparts, was regularly involved in war crimes throughout the conflict on the Eastern Front. On a number of occasions the division was responsible for the massacre of Jews. Discipline also proved to be a problem with the violent mistreatment of Soviet prisoners and civilians, which often led to cold-blooded murder. Complaints were even raised by neighbouring German and Slovak divisions about looting by the 5th SS in the Mius river area.

The 3rd SS had an equally unsavoury reputation. In October 1939, after the Polish campaign, three SS *Totenkopfverbände* (SS-VT) concentration camp guard regiments, numbering some 6,500 men, formed the SS Division *Totenkopf* (motorised). This took part in the invasion of the West and was responsible for the La Paradis massacre. While recuperating in southern France in November 1942 after serving in Russia, it became the SS Panzergrenadier Division *Totenkopf* and on 22 October 1943 was redesignated a panzer division. During 1943 it had fought at Kharkov, Belgorod and Kursk.

The 3rd SS *Totenkopf* was notified to move north as early as 25 June 1944, but disruption to the rail networks and roads meant that it took two weeks to get to northeastern Poland. Arriving on 7 July, it found the Red Army was already striking towards the Polish city of Grodno, threatening the southern flank of Army Group Centre's 4th Army and the northern flank of 2nd Army.

Deployed to Grodno, the 3rd SS was assigned the task of creating a defensive line for 4th Army to retire behind. Spectacularly, the division held off 400 Soviet tanks for eleven days before withdrawing southwest towards Warsaw. Joined by the Hermann Göring Panzer Division at Siedlce, 50 miles east of the Polish capital, they held the Soviets for almost a week from 24 July, keeping open an escape corridor for 2nd Army as it fled towards the Vistula. Three days later the Soviets threw almost 500 tanks to the south and by the 29th were at the suburbs of Warsaw.

The 5th SS arrived in western Warsaw on 27 July and trundled through the city to take up positions to the east. The next day Stalin ordered General Rokossovsky to occupy Praga, Warsaw's suburbs on the eastern bank of the Vistula, and to establish a number of bridgeheads over the river to the south of the city. Rokossovsky at this stage enjoyed a three to one superiority in infantry and five to one in armour and artillery. His front had at its disposal nine armies. Against all this, Model's 2nd Army could muster four understrength panzer divisions and one infantry division, while 9th Army had just two divisions and two brigades of infantry. However, four panzer divisions, the 3rd SS, 5th SS, 4th and 19th, poised to counter-attack, now defended the approaches to the Polish capital.

The 5th SS struck in a westerly direction from Stanislawow with fifty panzers in an effort to link up with the Hermann Göring and 19th Panzer Divisions, then fighting a tank battle at Okuniew and Ossow. The panzers were repulsed and on the evening of the 31st the Soviets took Okuniew, but could not budge the Germans from their strongpoint at Ossow. North of the Soviet 8th Tank Corps, the 3rd Tank Corps remained unsupported and, like the 16th Corps, had endured a day of heavy attacks from German armour, artillery and infantry. The commander of the Soviet 2nd Tank Army was in an impossible position: his units were enduring heavy casualties, he was short of supplies and his rear was under threat.

Rokossovsky simply could not fulfil his orders to break through the German defences and enter Praga by 8 August; it was simply not possible. On the 1st at 1610 hours he ordered the attack to be broken off just as Model launched his major counter-attack. Model began to probe the weak spot in Rokossovsky's line between Praga and Siedlce. His intention was to hit the Soviets in the flank and the rear, and soon the 39th Panzer Corps was counter-attacking the 3rd Tank Corps to the northeast of Warsaw and driving it back to Wolomin.

The 3rd SS and three other army panzer divisions were to strike south into the unsupported Soviet columns. From Wegrow, pushing towards Wolomin, came the 5th SS. At the same time the 3rd SS was launched into the fray from Siedlce towards Stanislawow with the intention of trapping those Soviet forces on the northeastern bank of the Dluga.

General Nikolaus von Vormann, appointed to command 9th Army, bringing up reinforcements from 2nd Army's reserves, also launched a counter-attack. Using units of the 5th SS and 3rd SS attacking from the forests to the east of Michalow, he drove the Soviet 8th Guards Tank Corps from Okuniew at 2100 hours on 1 August and linked up with 39th Panzer Corps from the west.

By 2 August the 19th Panzer Division, followed by the 4th Panzer Division, was in Radzymin and the Soviet 3rd Tank Corps was thrown back towards Wolomin. The following day the Hermann Göring Panzer Division rolled into Wolomin. Vedeneev's 3rd Tank Corps was trapped in the city. Attempts by the 8th Guards Tank Corps and the 16th Tank Corps to reach them failed, with the 8th Guards suffering serious casualties in the attempt.

After a week of heavy fighting the Soviet 3rd Tank Corps was surrounded by the 4th and 19th Panzer Divisions; in the fighting, some 3,000 Soviet troops were killed and another 6,000 captured. The Soviets also lost 425 of the 808 tanks and self-propelled guns with which they had begun the battle on 18 July. By noon on the 5th the Germans had ceased their counter-attack and the battle for the Praga approaches had come to an end.

The 3rd Tank Corps was destroyed and the 8th Guards Tank Corps and the 16th Tank Corps had suffered major losses. The exhausted Soviet 2nd Tank Army handed over its positions to the 47th and 70th Armies and withdrew to lick its wounds. With the Wehrmacht fully tied up fending off Soviet attacks, it was left to Himmler's hated SS police units to stamp out the Polish rising.

A motley battle group of 12,000 troops under SS-Gruppenführer Heinz Reinefarth, supported by thirty-seven assault guns and a company of heavy tanks, was also assembled to crush the Polish Home Army in Warsaw. SS reinforcements included SS-Brigadeführer Kaminski's hated anti-partisan Russian National Liberation Army (*Russkaia Osvoboditelnania Norodnaia Armiia* – SS-Sturmbrigade RONA). This was also known as the 29th Waffen-Grenadier Division der SS and was one of the worst SS units ever created. Kaminski was supported by SS-Oberführer Oskar Dirlewanger's equally appalling anti-partisan brigade designated the 36th Waffen-Grenadier Division der SS. Both were little better than ill-disciplined militia.

General Heinz Guderian, Chief of the General Staff, was appalled by the conduct of Kaminski and Dirlewanger's men:

> Some of the SS units involved – which incidentally were not drawn from the Waffen-SS – failed to preserve their discipline. The Kaminski Brigade was composed of former prisoners of war, mostly Russians who were ill-disposed towards the Poles; the Dirlewanger brigade was formed from German convicts on probation. These doubtful units were now committed to desperate street battles where each house had to be captured and where the defendants were fighting for their lives; as a result they abandoned all moral standards.

By 26 August the 3rd SS had been forced back to Praga, but a counter-attack by them on 11 September thwarted another Red Army attempt to link up with the trapped Polish Home Army. It was the 3rd SS and 5th SS who had the dubious honour of consigning Warsaw to two months of bloody agony. They were not, though, directly involved in the suppression of the Warsaw uprising.

After sixty-two days, and the loss of 15,000 dead and 25,000 wounded, the Polish Home Army surrendered in Warsaw on 2 October. Up to 200,000 civilians had also been killed in the needless orgy of destruction. The vengeful Himmler expelled the rest of the civilian population and ordered Warsaw to be flattened. The *Wiking* and *Totenkopf* Panzer Divisions were to remain on the Eastern Front until the end of the war. Both fought in Hungary against the Red Army in early 1945, then withdrew to Austria to surrender to the Americans.

In the summer of 1944 two SS panzer divisions, the 3rd SS *Totenkopf* and the 5th SS *Wiking* were instrumental in stopping the Red Army before Warsaw. This *Wiking* Panther has an extremely crude camouflage scheme that appears to be three-tone and was evidently hand-painted.

Wiking Panzergrenadiers outside Warsaw. The 5th SS deployed to the east of the city in late July 1944 and struck towards Wolomin.

Officers and men of the *Wiking* Division about to go into action. There seems to be some doubt over which route they should be taking. The division had a full battalion of Panthers at the start of the battle to hold Warsaw.

This Panzer IV Ausf H belongs to the 3rd SS Panzer Division *Totenkopf* and also has a three-tone camouflage, this time sprayed on. It lacks the Zimmerit anti-magnetic coating.

A Tiger I serving with the *Totenkopf* Division, photographed in 1944. *Totenkopf* deployed to Poland in late June 1944 but took two weeks to get to the northeast of the country.

The Panthers had to fend off Soviet tanks on the flat plain outside Warsaw that was ideal tank country. Operations by the Waffen-SS and German army resulted in the destruction of the Soviet 3rd Tanks Corps, with two other corps badly mauled.

Smiling Soviet troops examine a knocked-out Panther. The Red Army suffered a very serious defeat at Radzymin and Wolomin.

The soldiers of the Polish Home Army lacked heavy weapons to resist the Germans. The Warsaw Uprising commenced on 1 August 1944 but the tank battles fought east of the city ensured the Home Army was cut off for two months before being forced to surrender.

Polish fighters from the 'Czata 49' Battalion in the Wola district with British-supplied PIAT (Projector Infantry Anti-Tank) man-portable anti-tank weapons. Against panzers the PIAT had an effective range of about 115 yards but could manage three times that as an indirect fire weapon.

Polish fighters with the 'Zośka' Battalion supported by the 'Wacek' tank platoon using a captured Panther on the corner of Okopowa and Wolność Street.

The 'Zośka' Battalion employed two captured Panthers, both of which had been heavily damaged and had to be abandoned on 11 August 1944.

Wacław Micuta 'Wacek' commanded the Home Army's tank platoon. He is pictured here with one of the captured Panthers.

Polish Home Army troops from the 8th 'Krybar' Regiment with an SdKfz 251 captured from the 5th SS, photographed on 14 August 1944.

The Poles also had a single home-made armoured car built by supporters of the 'Krybar' Regiment using a Chevrolet 157 van. It was dubbed *Kubuś* or 'Little Jacob' by its crew and was armed with a machine gun and home-made flame-thrower. Miraculously it survived the war.

Members of Kaminski's hated SS-Sturmbrigade RONA in Warsaw. This ill-disciplined Russian militia was originally created for anti-partisan operations on the Eastern Front. The man on the right in the panzertruppen uniform with the POA arm shield is from the Russian Liberation Army, a separate organisation that came under the Army and not the SS.

Children examine a burnt-out Panzer IV destroyed in Warsaw in September 1944 during the uprising. It may have belonged to *Totenkopf*, though no divisional signs are visible.

Bronislav Kaminski and his men perpetrated the most appalling atrocities in Warsaw and he was swiftly disowned by both the Waffen-SS and the army. Himmler ordered his execution.

A unit of the Polish Home Army surrendering to the Germans in Warsaw on 5 October 1944. After the Red Army failed to reach them, their fate was sealed.

After the Warsaw uprising, most of the city was systematically flattened.

Chapter Six

Hohenstaufen's Arnhem Victory

After the defeat of the German Army and the Waffen-SS in Normandy in August 1944, Field Marshal von Rundstedt, CinC West, reported:

> At this time, about 100 tanks are combat ready in Army Group B. Enemy air force dominates the battle area and the lines of communication deep into the rear echelon.... Our task is to fight with available forces to gain time, to make the western positions and the Westwall [Siegfried Line] completely capable for defence.

Despite the developing Allied threat to the German city of Aachen, Hitler's intelligence judged that the Allies would strike towards Arnhem, which lay on the northern bank of the Dutch Rhine. A British 1st Airborne Division's intelligence summary noted, 'It is reported that one of the broken panzer divisions has been sent back to the area north of Arnhem to rest and refit; this might produce some 50 tanks.' SS-Obergruppenführer Wilhelm 'Willi' Bittrich and his exhausted 2nd SS Panzer Corps had indeed been withdrawn to the Netherlands, having successfully escaped the envelopment at Falaise.

Bittrich did not know that his *Hohenstaufen* and the *Frundsberg* SS Panzer Divisions were in the path of a major Allied airborne and ground attack, which was designed to 'bounce' the Rhine and overrun the vital industrial region of the Ruhr. He and his divisional commanders assumed that they were in a quiet sector to recuperate, so were not unduly alarmed at the poor condition of their units after the heavy fighting in France. Crucially they lacked both manpower and panzers.

Just four days before Operation Market Garden was scheduled to start, General 'Boy' Browning, commanding the British Airborne Corps, issued the following intelligence assessment: 'The total armoured strength is probably not more than 50–100 tanks ... There is every sign of the enemy strengthening the river and canal lines through Nijmegen and Arnhem . . . but the troops manning them are not numerous and many are of low category.'

It was at this stage that a fatal error of judgement occurred. In wartime, generals always have to make very difficult decisions, but on this occasion they grossly underestimated the capabilities of the Waffen-SS. Browning's intelligence was uncannily accurate. Bittrich's command accounted for less than a third of the estimated total, but just across the German border about sixty Tiger I and II tanks were on call. The latter were almost impossible for the paras to deal with, armed as they were with 57mm (6-pounder) anti-tank guns, 75mm Pack Howitzers and PIAT man-portable anti-tank weapons. Their only hope was to lay down such a barrage of fire that it would be enough to persuade the alarmed Tiger crews to break off contact. Such action would require incredible courage. Elements of an assault gun company were also to be made available for the Waffen-SS defence of Arnhem. Altogether this would give Bittrich at least ninety tanks and assault guns.

In addition, although Bittrich's divisions were in a poor condition, in Normandy they had proved highly adept at putting together effective battle groups using battered front-line troops and rear echelon personnel such as clerks and cooks. So not only did the Allies underestimate the potential strength of the panzers that would oppose Market Garden, they also underestimated Bittrich's response. A slow response would obviously allow them to steal a lead over the German defenders. A swift response would contest the Allied advance every inch of the way and jeopardise the success of the operation at Arnhem. To make matters worse, knowledge of Bittrich's presence did not filter down to everyone. British glider pilot Alexander Morrison recalled 'a brief summary of the known troops in northern Holland which, incidentally, made no reference to the two depleted divisions of German armour in the Arnhem area!'

Along the coast, once the British were in Antwerp, the German 15th Army fell back to a bridgehead blocking the mouth of the Scheldt estuary, thereby barring the sea approach to Antwerp. Dogged German resistance resulted in the Allies wasting almost two months trying to secure the port and the Scheldt, and in the meantime much-needed supplies had to be driven across Europe from the French ports by the trucks of the 'Red Ball Express'. This meant that just to the south everything rested on the performance of Bittrich's exhausted panzer divisions.

Under SS-Obersturmbannführer Walter Harzer, the 9th SS Panzer Division *Hohenstaufen* had barely 6,000 men and around twenty tanks but not all these were operational. Nonetheless, the division still had large numbers of other armoured fighting vehicles, such as armoured cars and self-propelled guns, along with forty armoured personnel carriers to transport its tough panzergrenadiers. This meant that Harzer's division was still more than capable of undertaking mobile operations. Under SS-Gruppenführer Heinz Harmel, *Hohenstaufen*'s sister division, the 10th SS *Frundsberg*, was much weaker. It retained fewer than 3,500 men and hardly any tanks. However, Bittrich was soon to be reinforced by elements of a heavy tank battalion equipped with forty-five Tiger IIs, a company of fourteen Tiger Is and a company of ten assault guns.

Hohenstaufen was deployed in the triangle formed by Arnhem, Zutphen and Apeldoorn. It was due to return to Germany for a much-needed refit and had been ordered to hand over many of its vehicles to *Frundsberg*. Perhaps understandably, Harzer was not keen on surrendering his remaining resources and deliberately dragged the process out. The 9th SS had also despatched forces to support Kampfgruppe Walther, part of Student's 1st Parachute Army.

Allied intelligence confirmed the deployment of *Hohenstaufen* and *Frundsberg* to the Nijmegen and Arnhem area. This was backed up by aerial reconnaissance flights and intelligence from the Dutch resistance. No one, though, seemed overly concerned. Major Tony Hibbert of the British 1st Parachute Brigade attended a meeting with Major Brian Urquhart, the chief intelligence officer of the 1st Airborne Division, noting, 'He went to General Browning, and said that in his view the operation could not succeed, because of the presence of these two divisions.' Browning, with just a week to prepare, decided that the operation would go ahead.

On the ground, carrying out the Garden element, Lieutenant General Brian Horrock's British 30th Corps with the Guards Armoured Division was to drive up Highway 69, followed by the 43rd Wessex and 50th Northumbrian Infantry Divisions. He was to reach Eindhoven on the first day, Nijmegen on the second day and Arnhem by day four. However, the British 1st Airborne Division would end up on its own for ten gruelling days, thanks to Bittrich.

The bulk of the 1st Airborne Division landed around Arnhem on 17 September 1944 in complete ignorance of the presence of the SS armour. Harzer was having lunch with Captain Paul Gräbner, commander of the divisional reconnaissance battalion, when Bittrich called. His instruction was for *Hohenstaufen* to 'reconnoitre in the direction of Arnhem and Nijmegen'. Harzer turned to Gräbner and said, 'Now what are we going to do? The vehicles are dismantled and on the train.' These included forty vehicles from Gräbner's unit. 'How soon can you have the tracks and guns put back on?' Harzer asked his subordinate, who was in the middle of consuming his soup. 'We'll be ready to move within three to five hours,' replied Gräbner. 'Get it done in three,' ordered Harzer, as he headed for his HQ. Bittrich had swiftly set in motion the reconstitution of the very panzer divisions that Allied intelligence so readily dismissed.

After Bittrich was informed of the British airborne drop, he immediately called for the bridges at Nijmegen and Arnhem to be brought down to stop them falling into enemy hands, but Field Marshal Model refused, claiming that they would be needed for the counter-attack. Following some initial confusion, Bittrich's two divisions quickly cobbled together various battle groups.

At the same time, on 17 September the artillery of General Horrock's 30th Corps opened fire to support the initial advance of the Irish Guards on a two-tanks-wide front with infantry from the 231st Brigade from the 50th Northumbrian Division. The Guards broke out of their Meuse-Escaut canal bridgehead and rolled into the Netherlands at 1500 hours, some 45 minutes after the opening barrage and air attacks. They then ran into elements of two battalions of the 9th SS and two German parachute battalions. These were pushed aside.

The 9th SS, although preparing to transit home, quickly sent its reconnaissance battalion south over the Arnhem highway bridge towards Nijmegen. Another battle group sped westward towards Oosterbeek, where most of the 1st Airborne Division was located; this would prevent reinforcements reaching those British paratroops already in Arnhem. The following day Gräbner's unit, leaving some self-propelled guns to guard the southern approaches of the Nijmegen bridge, headed north to Elst. A column of twenty-two vehicles then attempted to force a crossing of the Arnhem bridge, the northern end of which was by now firmly in British hands. Half of Gräbner's vehicles were destroyed and the SS were driven off amidst a blaze of fire from the Paras' strongpoints. The bridge was left strewn with debris and burnt-out vehicles.

The 10th SS was also despatched to Nijmegen to hold the main bridges against Horrock's advancing armour; this was key to isolating and destroying the paratroops at Oosterbeek. However, with the Arnhem bridge in British hands, the bulk of the 10th SS forces were obliged to use the ferry at Pannerden, 8 miles southeast of Arnhem. 'It was 1100 hours on the morning of Thursday, 21 September,' according to Geoffrey Powell, a company commander with 4th Para Brigade, 'before the Irish Guards received orders to break through to Arnhem Bridge . . . Waiting for them were German infantry, by now well dug-in and supported by tanks and SP guns.'

'For three days now,' added Powell, 'the dogged resistance of Brigadeführer Harmel's SS troops, fighting in the Betuwe between Nijmegen and Arnhem, had slowed the pace of the British advance.'

Major Winrich Behr, serving General Krebs, Field Marshal Model's Chief of Staff, recalled their counter-attacks at Arnhem on the 20th:

> At dawn the heavy SS *Frundsberg* Mortar Section moved into position and blasted the Arnhem bridgehead. This was followed by a frontal attack by ten somewhat elderly tanks firing wildly but continuously, and supported by infantry keeping up a steady pounding of heavy machine-gun fire. The tanks were met by the very accurate fire of the British 6-pounder anti-tank guns; they slowed to a stop and then began to back away.

The Germans secured the bridge at Arnhem that day. In the Oosterbeek pocket Glider Pilot Louis Hagen was grateful that the 9th SS was not up to full strength:

'If there had not been a sprinkling of first-class and fanatical officers and NCOs in this division, no fight would have been possible. But even with the present state of affairs, it was ridiculous that they did not wipe us out within a few hours.' On the 24th *Hohenstaufen*, reinforced by Heavy Tank Battalion 506, consisting of some forty-five powerful King IIs, set about eliminating the trapped defenders at Oosterbeek. Luckily for the Paras these attacks were initially poorly coordinated, with the panzers often operating without adequate infantry support, which left them vulnerable.

Frundsberg was eventually forced back, so Bittrich sent Tiger IIs and a company of Panthers to reinforce it, following the landing of the Polish 1st Parachute Brigade at Driel, south of Oosterbeek. Geoffrey Powell recalled how, 'defeated at Nijmegen, the 10th SS Panzer Division had retired towards Arnhem and was now waiting for 30th Corps' next move.' Horrocks' continually delayed tanks simply could not get through and on the 26th the difficult decision was taken to evacuate the exhausted paratroops trapped at Oosterbeek back across the Rhine. The remains of the British 1st Airborne Division escaped, leaving behind 1,485 dead and 6,414 captured. Bittrich's Waffen-SS panzer divisions suffered 3,300 casualties in stopping Market Garden from reaching its final objective.

The 9th SS and 10th SS Divisions successfully helped thwart Montgomery's attempt to end the war with a thrust into the Ruhr and the Allies reverted to their broad-front strategy across the whole of western Europe. Following its performance at Arnhem *Hohenstaufen* was sent to Paderborn for a well-earned break and to be re-equipped. Just after Arnhem *Frundsberg* was to cause yet more trouble. While trying to destroy the German salient at Geilenkirchen on 15 November 1944, elements of the British 43rd (Wessex) Infantry Division were trapped by the 10th SS around Hoven.

After Normandy, the weakened 2nd SS Panzer Corps withdrew to the Arnhem area in the Netherlands to recuperate. By September 1944 Walter Harzer, commanding the 9th SS Panzer Division *Hohenstaufen*, had about 6,000 men and twenty tanks available.

Members of the *Hohenstaufen* Division stocktaking personal effects next to their SdKfz 251. They are wearing the short-waisted M44 field blouse that was similar to the British Army's battle dress; the matching trousers were held up by a belt instead of braces. The blouse was made from Zeltbahn material with printed camouflage, which was originally designed as a wet weather poncho and pup tent.

Heinz Harmel's 10th SS *Frundsberg* had just 3,500 troops and a handful of tanks. Nonetheless the presence of the 2nd SS Panzer Corps at Arnhem ensured the failure of Operation Market Garden.

Möbelwagen self-propelled anti-aircraft guns belonging to *Hohenstaufen* at Arnhem; such armoured fighting vehicles were deadly against the lightly equipped British 1st Airborne Division.

Men of the British 1st Airborne Division landed at Arnhem little realising they would be facing German Tiger tanks and assault guns.

German debris on the northern ramp of Arnhem bridge following the counter-attack by the 9th SS on 18 September. It would take the Germans two days to recapture the bridge, cutting off the bulk of the 1st Airborne Division to the west at Oosterbeek.

Men from the 9th SS Panzer Division *Hohenstaufen* under guard by paras of the British 1st Airborne Division inside the Arnhem perimeter. They are wearing the four-pocket camouflage tunic modelled on the M1944 field uniform. Although it was forbidden to wear insignia on camouflage clothing, they have visible arm-eagles. The man second from the left wears a single button M1943 field cap with the standard woven death's-head insignia.

A StuG III from Sturmgeschütz Brigade 280 supporting troops from the 9th SS in Arnhem on 19 September 1944. Note the Schürzen side-skirts and Zimmerit anti-magnetic coating.

Hohenstaufen troops and their supporting assault guns on the streets of Arnhem. Initially, coordination between the two units was poor, leaving the assault guns very vulnerable to attack by British paratroops.

Sturmgeschütz Brigade 280 was en route to Aachen when ten of its assault guns (seven StuG IIIs and three StuH42s) were redeployed to assist 2nd SS Panzer Corps' operations.

Defiant-looking British paratroops being rounded up by *Hohenstaufen* troops on 20 September 1944 under the watchful eye of a StuG III crew.

SS Panzer IV destroyed by the 1st Parachute Brigade near Arnhem Bridge.

A well camouflaged Sturmhaubitze 42 (StuG III armed with a 105mm howitzer) belonging to StuG Brigade 280, obscured by a British parachute in Arnhem.

Another shot of a Sturmhaubitze 42, possibly the same vehicle, in Arnhem. Three of these were made available to the *Hohenstaufen* Division.

Schwere Panzer Kompanie 'Hummel' was sent to help the SS at Arnhem on 19 September. Although fourteen Tiger I tanks were despatched, part of the journey had to be completed by road and only two arrived in an operational condition. These two attacked Arnhem while the rest, once repaired, were sent over the bridge the following day to block Horrock's 30th Corps.

Hohenstaufen SdKfz 250 half-track in action against the paras at Oosterbeek.

Paras' 75mm Pack Howitzer firing in defence of the shrinking Oosterbeek perimeter. This weapon, plus the 6-pounder anti-tank gun and PIAT man-portable anti-tank weapon, provided the only defence against the panzers.

Schwere Panzer Abteilung 506, which had been re-equipping with Tiger IIs in Germany, was despatched to Arnhem on 24 September 1944. One company was attached to *Hohenstafen* to assist in attacking those British paratroops still holding out in the Oosterbeek pocket. A second company was sent to help the *Frundsberg* Division south of the Rhine at Elst.

A Tiger II knocked out in Oosterbeek on 25 September 1944; it took a 6-pounder anti-tank gun, a 75mm Pack Howitzer and a PIAT to finish it off. Fortunately this deterred the rest of the company from entering the pocket, otherwise a massacre could have occurred.

Another Tiger II destroyed during the fighting in the Netherlands. Although well armed and well armoured, its bulk made it unwieldy.

Chapter Seven

Dietrich's Autumn Mist

In late September 1944 the Allies became aware that Hitler was withdrawing his armour from the front in order to build up a very large panzer reserve. Alarmingly his tank strength on the Western Front steadily expanded to 2,600 tanks compared to 1,500 on the Eastern Front. Signals intelligence indicated that the 1st SS, 2nd SS, 9th SS and 12th SS Panzer Divisions, along with the 17th SS Panzergrenadier Division, were being refitted for renewed combat. Most notably, the two SS Panzer Corps were swiftly rebuilt as the strike force of SS-Oberstgruppenführer 'Sepp' Dietrich's powerful 6th SS Panzer Army. This was never officially designated an 'SS' army as it also included regular army divisions, but as it was led by the Waffen-SS it was considered as such.

The two panzer divisions of SS-Gruppenführer Hermann Priess' 1st SS Panzer Corps were each brought up to about 22,000 men; the 1st SS Panzer Division was supplemented with Tiger tanks of SS Heavy Panzer Battalion 502; and the 12th SS, now under SS-Brigadeführer Hugo Krass, was rebuilt, though it lacked experienced junior officers. The 2nd SS, reassigned to SS-Gruppenführer Heinz Lammerding, and the 9th SS, reassigned to SS-Brigadeführer Sylvester Stadler, of SS-Obergruppenführer Willi Bittrich's 2nd SS Panzer Corps were similarly rebuilt with better than average recruits, though the 9th SS lacked transport.

Up until the end of the year the 2nd SS and 10th SS Panzer Divisions helped hold the Siegfried Line while Hitler built up his counter-attack force for the Ardennes offensive, which had been in preparation from October. This was initially codenamed Watch on the Rhine (Wacht am Rhein) to imply a purely defensive operation, but subsequently became Autumn Mist (Herbstnebel). Planning was entrusted to Field Marshal Model's Army Group B and he was allocated the very last of Germany's reserves – some ten panzer and fourteen infantry divisions.

After three months the Americans had been unable to punch through the Siegfried Line between Geilenkirchen and Aachen. On 12/13 November the weak 17th SS and 21st Panzer Divisions counter-attacked at Sanry-sur-Nied, driving the Americans back, although they were forced to withdraw for fear of encirclement. The 17th SS was ordered to retreat and escaped being trapped in Metz, which finally fell on 17 November. By the beginning of December the division was down to just 4,000 men and twenty tanks and was no longer available for the Ardennes offensive.

Hitler's massed armed forces included Dietrich's 6th SS Panzer Army, with the 1st SS, 2nd SS, 9th SS and 12th SS Panzer Divisions, 501 and 506 Heavy Panzer Battalions, plus seven army divisions equipped with a total of 450 tanks, assault guns and self-propelled guns; von Manteuffel's 5th Panzer Army with nine divisions included about 350 armoured fighting vehicles. The 7th Army, with a similar number of divisions under General Erich Brandenberger, had a few battalions of tanks and assault guns. Antwerp was their goal; 6th SS Panzer Army was to break out between Liège and Aachen and 5th Panzer Army between Namur and Liège.

In the past Himmler had accepted SS divisions coming under army corps commanders and SS army corps and SS armoured groups coming under army commanders, but the Ardennes was a subordination of a completely different magnitude. For the first time a whole army was placed under the command of an SS general with the minority of his command consisting of SS units. This general, though, was under an army field marshal. Furthermore, the Waffen-SS was completely reliant on the army's newly raised Volksgrenadier divisions and Luftwaffe parachute units fighting as infantry to first seize the ground over which their panzers were to advance.

On 10 December 1944 Hitler found a convenient way to avoid Himmler being involved in the forthcoming Ardennes offensive. The Reichsführer-SS was appointed commander-in-chief of Army Group Upper Rhine, far from the centre of action. This meant he could not meddle in Field Marshal von Rundstedt's control of the 6th SS Panzer Army. Rundstedt as CinC West had been particularly irked by Himmler styling himself 'Supreme Commander, Westmark'. It also forced Himmler to commit his Replacement Army to the front; in particular, he plugged a gap in the defences of the German frontier south of Karlsruhe, which was independent of Rundstedt's command.

Although the Ardennes was the first time an SS army took to the field, only four of 'Sepp' Dietrich's six panzer divisions actually belonged to the Waffen-SS and two of them were soon detached from the right flank to bolster the 15th Army; they were replaced by the inadequate Volksgrenadier divisions of Himmler's Replacement Army. Dietrich, who nominally answered to von Rundstedt, was flabbergasted at the scope of the proposed operation:

> Reach the Meuse in two days, cross it, take Brussels, go on and then take Antwerp? Simple. As if my tanks could advance in a bog. And this little programme is to be executed in the depths of winter in a region where there

are nine chances out of ten that we will have snow up to our middles. Do you call that serious?

He hoped to reason with Hitler but the Führer would not see him. Dietrich was acutely aware that although the SS panzer divisions had been rebuilt, they were not what they had once been, bitterly observing: 'Out of all the original Adolf Hitler Division there are only thirty men today who are not dead or prisoners. Now I have recreated a new panzer army and I am a general and not an undertaker.'

Perhaps not surprisingly after its losses in Normandy, the 12th SS was only able to field one mixed tank battalion for the Ardennes offensive, consisting of two companies of Panzer IVs and two companies of Panthers. The other battalion remained in Germany, where it was being reconstituted. The division also committed its two panzergrenadier regiments and its anti-tank battalion. Kampfgruppe Peiper, drawn from the 1st SS, consisted of a hundred Panzer IVs and Panthers, forty-two formidable King Tigers and twenty-five assault guns.

Elements of the 1st SS and 12th SS Panzer Divisions conducted the 6th SS Panzer Army's main attacks to the north along the line St Vith–Vielsalm on 16 December 1944. They did so under dense cloud, thereby avoiding the unwanted attentions of the Allies' troublesome fighter-bombers.

Unfortunately for Dietrich, SS-Obersturmbannführer Peiper, whose forces were desperately short of fuel, turned north to seize 50,000 gallons of American gasoline at Bullingen, instead of pushing west. His force was eventually surrounded and destroyed, leaving forty-five tanks and sixty self-propelled guns north of the Ambleve river.

The 12th SS, following-up the Kampfgruppe, was unable to dislodge the Americans from the Elsenborn Ridge and had to swing left, nor was Panzer Lehr able to get to Bastogne before the Americans reinforced the town. On the northern shoulder of the advance the 9th SS headed northward after breaking through the Losheim Gap; frustratingly only the artillery regiment and reconnaissance battalion were committed, although once St Vith was captured the rest of the division was brought in. On 18 December the troops of the 9th SS reached their official start line and fought their way towards Manhay and Trois Ponts before being replaced by the 12th Volksgrenadier Division. They got as far as Salmchateau, less than halfway to the Meuse.

Meanwhile 116th Panzer drove between Bastogne and St Vith, but the Americans holding out in Bastogne delayed 2nd Panzer. Crucially, the failure to take Bastogne greatly slowed Manteufell's drive on the Meuse. St Vith fell on 21 December, though American artillery fire forced the 6th SS Panzer Army to become entangled with the 5th Panzer Army. Hitler felt that even if Antwerp were not taken, keeping his panzers in the hard-won bulge created in the front line would slow the Allies' push on the vital Ruhr. To secure the bulge, Bastogne had to be taken and the 12th SS was shifted south to help capture the town.

By 22 December the 9th SS had been committed to the southern flank of the 1st SS, but could not reach Kampfgruppe Peiper. At the end of the month the 9th SS was replaced by the 12th Infantry Division and also moved south to help with the assault on Bastogne. However, once the weather cleared Allied fighter-bombers began to attack the exposed panzers in a repeat of the Falaise battle. Exposed on the snow-covered landscape, many were easy targets. Lacking fuel, 2nd Panzer got as far as Celles, just 4 miles short of the river Meuse, before American armour moved in. American tanks also halted the 2nd SS, while 116th and Panzer Lehr were stopped short of Marche.

Even in the face of defeat, the 2nd SS continued to inflict heavy losses on the Americans. Normandy survivor Untersturmführer Fritz Langanke took his Panther tank into battle just before Christmas:

> Thanks to our preparations, we knocked out the first five Sherman tanks in quick succession, despite the poor visibility. They moved at a steep angle to us, down the slope, half-right. The firing distance between us was 500 and 700 metres. The other tanks then turned around and drove back. Thereafter it was quiet and dusk set in soon.

The US 6th Armored Division launched an attack near Bastogne on 2 January 1945. Although the tanks were driven off, American infantry broke through the positions of the 26th Volksgrenadier Division, reaching Michamps. Under Normandy survivor von Ribbentrop, the 12th SS escort company and the 1st Battalion, SS Panzer Regiment 12, were sent to counter-attack. They recaptured Michamps and Obourcy, and along with the fighting at Arlencourt the 12th SS accounted for twenty-four American tanks. The 12th SS was then thrown at the northeast outskirts of Bastogne on the 4th, but the Americans turned back every attack. Shortly afterwards the 12th SS was withdrawn to Cologne. By now the 9th and 12th SS Panzer Divisions only had fifty-five tanks left between them.

During the New Year Dietrich was dismayed that his SS panzer divisions had been handed over to the army to help take Bastogne. First *Leibstandarte* then the whole of the 1st SS Panzer Corps were assigned to Manteuffel. By 4 January *Hohenstaufen* had also been reassigned, leaving Dietrich with just *Das Reich* as his sole armoured unit. Within four days both generals were in full retreat, heading back to their start line. Rundstedt counselled Hitler to withdraw the two battered panzer armies east of Bastogne ready for the inevitable Allied counter-attack. On 8 January

Hitler finally ordered a partial withdrawal. The 6th SS Panzer Army was now needed on the Eastern Front following a major Soviet offensive.

Meanwhile Himmler, with his first combat command, wanted to launch a major offensive across the Rhine. In order to distract attention from the Ardennes, he conducted Operation Northwind (*Nordwind*) to the south in Alsace, involving ten divisions, including the Normandy veterans 10th SS Panzer and 17th SS Panzergrenadier on 31 December. It was simply too late to have any bearing on the fighting in the Ardennes.

Undoubtedly for Himmler this was a matter of SS prestige over the army. While the Army High Command had floundered on the Ardennes battlefield, Himmler believed he could be the conqueror of Alsace if he could retake Strasbourg. He wanted to be the civilian who had won a victory defending Germany while the army had failed. This conveniently avoided the embarrassing truth that 'Sepp' Dietrich and the 6th SS Panzer Army had also failed, even if it had been under the direction of the army.

Himmler's planning was flawed from the start, because his offensive was to comprise three generally unrelated local offensives that could be contained piecemeal. His SS staff dominating Army Group Upper Rhine proposed a swift advance to the Saverne Gap by three panzer divisions, including the 10th SS supported by Volksgrenadier divisions to the north and south. This would cut the US 7th Army in two, the southern portion of which would then be destroyed, allowing Himmler's offensive to sweep the French Army out of Strasbourg.

Along with the 36th Volksgrenadier Division, the 17th SS Panzergrenadiers attacked the US 44th and 100th Infantry Divisions near Rimlingen on 1 January 1945. Within a week they had been thrown back and the Americans recaptured Rimlingen on the 13th. It was only after the Americans had withdrawn in good order towards the River Moder south of the Forêt de Haguenau that Himmler launched his secondary attacks in the centre around Gambsheim and to the south around Erstein.

The 10th SS achieved some success in its attack from Offendorf to Herlisheim on 17 January. Although this lost momentum, Obersturmführer Bachmann, adjutant of the 1st Battalion, SS Panzer Regiment 10, remembered:

> Everything went according to plan. The two-panzer crew cooperated in a first-rate fashion. Panzer 2 opened fire while Panzer 1 raced into the junction and knocked out the first Sherman. More US tanks were knocked out, and a white flag appeared. . . .
>
> The total was twelve captured Sherman tanks and sixty prisoners. I deployed my own two Panthers forward to the edge of Herlisheim. From

> there they covered in the direction of Drusenheim and knocked out two Shermans on their way to Herlisheim. Thus my two Panthers achieved nine kills.

Bachmann's tanks crews were rewarded with Iron Crosses, with Bachmann himself gaining the Knight's Cross. This success posed a threat to Strasbourg, forcing the Allies to counter-attack and clear the Germans from the west bank of the Rhine. Although Himmler's Operation Northwind caused a small crisis for the Allies, it also wasted away Hitler's already meagre reserves.

By the end of January, Hitler's Ardennes bulge had gone for the loss of 100,000 casualties and most of their armour; the 5th Panzer Army and the 6th SS Panzer Army lost up to 600 tanks. Hitler's great gamble had not paid off, although in five weeks of fighting twenty-seven American divisions suffered 59,000 casualties thanks to his reconstituted panzer divisions.

However, Hitler had achieved what Falaise had failed to do: the near-total destruction of the panzer forces in the West. This time there could be no miraculous recovery. Rundstedt did all he could to make the Waffen-SS shoulder the blame for the failure of the Ardennes offensive: 'I received few reports from "Sepp" Dietrich of the 6th [SS] Panzer Army and what I did receive was generally a pack of lies. If the SS had any problems, they reported them directly to the Führer.'

In late January 1945 Himmler was posted to the Eastern Front to command Army Group Vistula. General Westphal, one of Himmler's bitterest critics, regarded his organisational abilities as a shambles. Upon Himmler's departure, 'There was naturally no question of an orderly transfer,' wrote Westphal, as the Reichsführer-SS left behind 'a laundry-basket full of unsorted orders and reports.'

Paul Hausser assumed command of the Upper Rhine, which came under Rundstedt as CinC West. Hausser found himself with the unenviable task of holding the Colmar pocket with much-depleted forces. Himmler took with him General Lammerding as his Chief of Staff. Lammerding, former commander of the 2nd SS *Das Reich*, had blood of the Oradour-sur-Glane massacre and the Tulle executions on his hands. Himmler did not care.

Leibstandarte Hummels from the 1st SS Artillery Regiment being shipped to the front. The 1st SS Panzer Division deployed with the 6th SS Panzer Army's 1st SS Panzer Corps under Hermann Priess.

At the end of 1944 SS-Oberstgruppenführer 'Sepp' Dietrich's 6th SS Panzer Army was tasked to take part in Operation Autumn Mist, Hitler's surprise offensive in the Ardennes. Dietrich was aghast at the idea of trying to reach Antwerp.

A Waffen-SS StuG III being manoeuvred into position; note the captured American half-track to the left. Kampfgruppe Peiper, drawn from *Leibstandarte*, included such assault guns. By late November 1944 *Das Reich* and *Hohenstaufen* had two companies of StuGs instead of Panzer IVs.

The initial German advance into the heavily wooded Ardennes on 16 December 1944 caught the US Army completely by surprise. Here Waffen-SS panzergrenadiers riding in an SdKfz 251 pass an abandoned American M3 half-track. The vehicle in the middle of the road is a Panzer IV Möbelwagen self-propelled 37mm anti-aircraft gun.

The classic Battle of the Bulge shot – *Leibstandarte* SS panzergrenadiers of Kampfgruppe Hansen passing abandoned American equipment on 18 December 1944. This was what remained of Task Force Mayes from the US 14th Cavalry Group. The man on the right is carrying a captured American M1 carbine.

Another *Leibstandarte* SS panzergrenadier who was photographed in the same Kampfgruppe Hansen sequence. He is an MG42 gunner, with his loader just behind him.

Shocked American PoWs taken at Stoumont by Kampfgruppe Peiper on 19 December 1944.

A Panther roaring through the forests of the Ardennes in late December 1944. The powerful 6th SS Panzer Army was thwarted in bringing its strength to bear by the onset of bad weather and the difficult terrain. Only the lead elements were able to pierce the American positions. Ironically, the deepest penetration was not by the Waffen-SS but by the army's 2nd Panzer Division.

A Sherman from the US 2nd Armored Division rumbles past an abandoned Panther Ausf G near Grandmenil, just to the west of Manhay. It is covered in a layer of snow and appears undamaged, so may have been abandoned for lack of fuel. American troops can be seen digging foxholes in the background.

American victims of the Malmedy massacre. They were shot by members of Kampfgruppe Peiper, and responsibility for this atrocity rested firmly on the Waffen-SS.

An abandoned Tiger II. Kampfgruppe Peiper included twenty Tiger IIs belonging to Schwere SS Panzer Abteilung 501. The Tiger II was much too heavy and proved a liability in the Ardennes – half a dozen were lost in and around La Geize and another three at Stavlot.

Captured *Hitlerjugend*. The 12th SS was commanded by Hugo Krass for the Ardennes offensive and was reputedly 22,000 strong but lacked experienced junior officers.

American M36 tank destroyers moving through the bad weather to counter-attack. This Gun Motor Carriage had only recently entered service with the US Army and could knock out both the Panther and Tiger at long range thanks to its powerful 90mm anti-tank gun. An M36 helped block Kampfgruppe Peiper at Stoumont and M36s of the US 613th Tank Destroyer Battalion helped stop the 12th SS at the southern end of the Elsenborn ridge.

An abandoned *Das Reich* Kubelwagen. The 2nd SS Panzer Division had been rebuilt during the autumn with replacements that were considered better than average.

A knocked-out Panther in the Ardennes. The 5th Panzer Army and the 6th SS Panzer Army lost up to 600 tanks. The latter unit was not given time to recover as Hitler immediately packed it off to Hungary.

Belgian civilians massacred by the Germans during the ultimately futile Ardennes offensive.

The final resting place of a Jagdpanther left high and dry after the snows melted. Panzerjäger Abteiling 560, attached to *Hitlerjugend*, was equipped with the Jagdpanther. This unit took part in the attack on the twin villages of Krinkelt-Rocherath in a failed attempt to turn the Elsenborn ridge.

Chapter Eight

Himmler's Winter Solstice

After the failure of Hitler's Autumn Mist offensive, it was widely assumed that the remaining tanks of 'Sepp' Dietrich's 6th SS Panzer Army would be withdrawn east to help fend off the Red Army, which was encroaching over the Oder. Instead, much to his generals' dismay, Hitler decided they would be sent to Hungary to spearhead an attack there.* The defence of Berlin fell to Himmler's Army Group Vistula, which was cobbled together from the remains of two other army groups.

Deep down the Reichsführer-SS must have worried that the Waffen-SS's glory days were behind them – the failure of his armoured divisions to gain victory in the Ardennes and Alsace had seen to that. Furthermore he must have been aware that he kept being sidelined and that his star within the Nazi hierarchy was waning.

The Soviet salient over the Oder was to be pinched off by simultaneous attacks conducted by Himmler in Pomerania and General Schoerner in Silesia. Rather optimistically, more than 1,200 panzers from the 3rd Panzer Army were earmarked for Operation Solstice (*Sonnenwende*). Even if such inflated numbers had been available, there were insufficient trains to move them and little or no fuel and ammunition. Also the 3rd Panzer Army was needed to hold the banks of the Oder to the north of the strategic Seelow Heights, which dominated the approaches to Berlin.

Himmler's attack was to be conducted by SS-Obergruppenführer Felix Steiner's newly created 11th SS Panzer Army, which consisted – on paper at least – of three corps. These included the *Nordland*, *Nederland* and *Wallonien* Waffen-SS divisions that had originated in Scandinavia and the Low Countries. This operation was to be one of the last major German armoured offensives on the Eastern Front and, like the attack in Hungary, was dominated by the SS.

Throughout January 1945 the 9th SS Panzer Division conducted a fighting withdrawal to the German border. It was then sent to the Kaufenheim-Mayen area to be re-equipped before going on to Hungary. The 10th SS, which had also faithfully served the 2nd SS Panzer Corps throughout the Normandy campaign, at Arnhem and the Ardennes offensive, was now detached from its sister division and sent to the Vistula sector. Its remaining thirty-eight Panzer IVs and fifty-three Panthers would

* For more on this operation, see the author's *The Battle for Budapest 1944-45*, also published by Pen & Sword Military.

not rejoin the 6th SS Panzer Army for Hitler's forthcoming Hungarian offensive. Instead they would spearhead Himmler's Operation Solstice.

Other Normandy SS veterans would also take part. Schwere SS Panzer Abteilung 502 (formerly 102) was refitted at Sennelager, while the 503's 1st Company moved to Bentfeld, the 2nd to Eilsen and the 3rd to Hovelhof. The Panzer Ersatz und Ausbildungs (training and replacement) Abteilung 500 at Paderborn provided much-needed crews and between 19 and 22 September 1944 503 received forty-five new Tiger IIs. The following month it was shipped to Hungary and subordinated to the Feldhernhalle Panzer Corps and assisted in the futile defence of Budapest.

Schwere Panzer Abteilung 503 was back in Germany by January 1945. It was split in two, with one group sent to the Arnswalde-Pomerania area and the other to the Landsberg-Küstrin area. Arnswalde's strategic position protecting Stargard and the sea port of Stettin meant that there was a strong German garrison defending the town. The first group under SS-Obersturmbannführer Fritz Herzig, along with a panzer support battalion, 1,000 troops and 5,000 civilians, was trapped in Arnswalde on 4 February. Herzig's Tiger II could have fought their way out but that would have meant abandoning everyone else to their fate. Three days later SS-Untersturmführer Fritz Kauerauf set out from Stargard with three Tiger IIs heading for Arnswalde via Reetz. He then became involved with the 11th SS trying to stop the Soviet advance to the Baltic.

On 13 February Chief of the General Staff General Heinz Guderian, along with 'Sepp' Dietrich, in conference with Hitler, advocated a pincer movement against the advancing Soviets in an attempt to keep open the German 2nd Army's lines of communication between East Prussia and Pomerania. To the displeasure of Himmler, who also attended, the SS attack was to be directed by Army General Walther Wenck, Guderian's second-in-command.

Guderian had great respect for the Waffen-SS panzer divisions:

> I fought with the *SS-Leibstandarte Adolf Hitler* and with the SS Division *Das Reich*: later as Inspector General of Armoured Troops, I visited numerous SS divisions. I can therefore assert that to my knowledge the SS divisions were always remarkable for a high standard of discipline, of *esprit de corps*, and conduct in the face of the enemy. They fought shoulder to shoulder with the panzer divisions of the Army, and the longer the war went on the less distinguishable they became from the Army.

Guderian felt that much of this professionalism was thanks to the work of former army general Paul Hausser. In contrast, he was not impressed by the Reichsführer-SS, stating: 'In military matters Himmler proved an immediate and total failure. His appreciation of our enemies was positively childish.'

Dietrich was aghast that his panzer army was being sent to Hungary; it made no sense in light of the imminent threat to Berlin. He also had a very personal reason to be against such a move, as his family were living near the Oder. Later Dietrich had them moved to safety at the Nazi *Ordensburg* at Sonthofen but at the time he was very worried. Having said his piece, he remained sullen and hostile for the rest of the meeting, while Hitler and Guderian argued over appointing Wenck as Himmler's chief of staff.

Guderian had no confidence in Himmler's own choice, General Heinz Lammerding, whom he considered merely a policeman and amateur divisional commander. Lammerding lasted as Himmler's chief of staff for just two months. Before becoming a divisional commander at the age of 39, he had served as chief of staff of the 3rd SS Panzer Division *Totenkopf* in Russia. He now found himself packing, having been sacked.

Initially Hitler stated that Himmler was 'man enough to carry out the attack on his own', but after two hours of arguing turned to an embarrassed Reichsführer-SS and said 'Very well, Himmler, Wenck is coming to you this evening and will take charge. The attack begins on the 15th.'

It was decided to relieve Arnswalde and attack in the Landsberg-Küstrin area. The 10th SS and half a dozen other Waffen-SS divisions, serving with Steiner's 39th Panzer, 3rd (Germanische) SS Panzer and 10th SS Army Corps, were to take part in the counter-attack on Marshal Georgi Zhukov's advancing 1st Belorussian Front.

Himmler, regardless of the military situation, felt completely humiliated and retired to hospital at Hohenlychen. He knew that the Waffen-SS had been taken away from him, and perhaps he also finally appreciated that he was not fit to command. From Hohenlychen he 'bravely' issued the order of the day exhorting the Waffen-SS 'Forward through the mud! Forward through the snow! Forward by day! Forward by night! Forward to the liberation of German soil!' The truth was that Himmler had no actual military aptitude and had always been reliant on SS generals such as 'Willi' Bittrich, 'Sepp' Dietrich and Paul Hausser to secure his victories that impressed Hitler so much.

In the event, elements of just four weak SS 'armoured' divisions, comprising the 4th SS *Polizei*, the 11th SS Freiwilligen Panzergrenadier *Nordland*, the 23rd SS Panzergrenadier *Nederland* and the 10th SS Panzer, plus around four army divisions, were thrown into the short-lived attack on the 15th between Stargard and Arnswalde. The 4th SS had mainly been on security duties up to this point and the 10th SS was exhausted by the constant combat.

Nordland at the start of the year included a powerful armoured unit, the SS Panzer Battalion Herman von Salza, and was a well equipped full-strength division. After constant battles along the Baltic, it had been considerably weakened. *Nederland* was a paper division and only of brigade strength. Many of its men were lost when their transport ship *Moira* was sunk en route to Danzig. Two SS grenadier divisions were also involved, including the 28th *Wallonien*. Between them these forces could muster fewer than 300 panzers and tank destroyers. Almost 10,000 infantry allocated to the operation were still en route from Norway when *Sonnenwende* started.

Steiner's so-called 11th SS Panzer Army, led by *Nordland*, initially made good progress on the first day, penetrating the Soviet envelopment of Arnswalde and rescuing the German garrison. The following day the rest of the 3rd (Germanische) SS Panzer Corps fought to enlarge the corridor. However, the panzers and the infantry were on their own as they had hardly any air cover from the Luftwaffe or artillery support. It was only a matter of time before the Red Army and Red Air Force recovered and responded.

Panzer Abteilung 503's Tiger IIs were instrumental in holding the corridor open as the wounded and civilians were evacuated and fresh troops sent in. During the fighting in the Danzig-Gotenhafen area Tigers of 503 destroyed sixty-four Soviet tanks, and Soviet troops were expelled from Brallentin and two villages. The Germans then cut into Marshal Bogdanov's 2nd Tank Army to retake Pyritz. However, by this stage of the war the Tiger's dominance of the battlefield was no longer assured.

The 11th SS Panzer Army's short-lived success swiftly came to a halt in the face of the Red Army's superior firepower. Although the Tiger II was armed with an even more powerful 88mm gun than the Tiger I, the Joseph Stalin tank was more than a match for it. The IS-2 heavy tank carried a 122mm gun and the previous year had proved itself a worthy adversary for the Tiger. On one occasion the previous summer a force of eleven IS-2s mauled a force of fourteen Tiger IIs, destroying four and damaging another seven for the loss of three tanks and seven damaged.

The Tigers could do little once the 2nd Soviet Guards Tank Army brought up heavy Joseph Stalin tanks on 17 February. In addition, as the frost thawed, the ground began to turn to mud, which the wide tracks of the Soviet tanks were better able to cope with. On the same day Wenck, returning from Hitler's evening briefing, was injured in a car crash and the momentum of the operation was completely lost.

Steiner called off the assault, pulling his 3rd (Germanische) SS Panzer Corps back to the Stargard and Stettin area on the northern Oder river. The few remaining panzers were moved to the Oder front. The least damaged unit, the 4th SS *Polizei* Panzergrenadier Division, was shipped by sea to help in the defence of Danzig before being sent to Berlin.

By the 19th the Red Army had recaptured Arnswalde, surrounded Graudenze and destroyed the German base at Stargard. The ill-conceived Operation *Sonnenwende* cost Himmler's Army Group Vistula considerable casualties among the few SS divisions that could still be relied on to conduct organised counter-attacks.

In reality this attack was little more than a nuisance to the Red Army. Hitler and Himmler achieved nothing save grinding down those few units still capable of conducting offensive operations on the Eastern Front. For the forthcoming battle of Berlin the discredited Reichsführer-SS found himself replaced by Colonel-General Gotthard Heinrici as the commander of Army Group Vistula.

Nonetheless, the Stargard operation caused enough alarm in the Red Army for them to halt the main offensive towards Berlin, and they lost some six valuable weeks while they cleared Pomerania of enemy forces. Steiner's actions at Arnswalde also convinced Hitler that he was the man to rescue Berlin in late April 1945 – but Steiner, with just 11,000 men, refused to obey orders, much to Hitler's fury. After the failure of Dietrich's 6th SS Panzer Army in the Ardennes and Hungary, in Hitler's mind Steiner's insubordination was the final betrayal by the Waffen-SS. The Führer even threatened Steiner with death but it did no good: Steiner's loyalty was to his surviving men.

At the end of 1944 Himmler found himself CinC Army Group Upper Rhine. This appointment was designed to stop him meddling with the Ardennes offensive. Instead he conducted Operation Northwind in Alsace, using the 10th SS Panzer Division *Frundsberg* and the 17th SS Panzergrenadier Division *Götz von Berlichingen*.

Frundsberg Panther Ausf Gs in winter camouflage in Alsace. These tanks seem to have a very dark base colour, and there is some indication that *dunkel grau* was reintroduced in late 1944 for front-line armour. Himmler's attack in mid-January 1945 achieved limited success before losing momentum, and had no impact on the Battle of the Bulge.

Another Panther moving through concrete dragon's teeth forming part of the Siegfried Line or Westwall for the attack in Alsace. It has the same zig-zag whitewash winter camouflage.

A burning SdKfz 251 lost in the fighting during the winter of 1944/45. It still has its summer/autumn camouflage scheme. Most of the Waffen-SS vehicles used in the Ardennes and Alsace operations were not whitewashed.

Whitewashed StuG III assault guns belonging to the *Wiking* Division on their way from Warsaw to Budapest to take part in Hitler's Hungarian offensive in early 1945. After the Ardennes, it was anticipated that Dietrich's 6th SS Panzer Army would be sent to hold the Oder but instead it was deployed to Hungary.

Totenkopf SS panzergrenadiers in winter parkas, with an SdKfz 251 and amphibious Schimmwagen, photographed in January 1945 during the fighting in Hungary to relieve the trapped Budapest garrison.

Late in the war SdKfz 251/22 consisted of the 251 half-track armed with the PaK40 75mm anti-tank gun. These were built on Hitler's orders in a desperate attempt to provide as many self-propelled anti-tank guns as possible. They were issued to the panzer divisions in 1945 with nine sent to the panzerjäger detachments, three to the reconnaissance detachments and six to the gun platoons. This example has an army prefaced number plate.

In mid-February 1945 Felix Steiner's so-called 11th SS Panzer Army, consisting of half a dozen Waffen-SS divisions, was thrown into a counter-attack (Operation Solstice) against the Red Army to relieve German forces trapped at Arnswalde.

Another Panther Ausf G in winter camouflage very similar to that used by the *Frundsberg* Division. It has the late war gun mantlet with the flat lower edge shot deflector. Steiner's attack involved four SS armoured divisions including the *Frundsberg*.

Heinz Harmel, commander of the *Frundsberg* Division, photographed in February 1945. To his left is Otto Paesh, commander of SS Panzer Regiment 10, and on his right Karl-Heinz Euling, one of his SS panzergrenadier regimental commanders.

Panthers and tank riders moving up for the attack. Steiner's six SS divisions could muster fewer than 300 panzers on 15 February 1945 but they managed to reach Arnswalde.

Tiger IIs from Schwere Panzer Abteilung 503 were instrumental in holding open the corridor to Arnswalde, but not many were available.

Three days after Operation Solstice commenced, the Red Army committed its powerful IS-2 heavy tanks. Armed with a massive 122mm gun, these were able to combat the Tiger II. Steiner had no option but to pull back his 11th SS Panzer Army, and Arnswalde and Stargard were lost.

Leibstandarte half-tracks in Hungary during Hitler's ill-fated Operation Spring Awakening, conducted in March 1945. This was the final defeat for the Waffen-SS.

A pair of wrecked Panzer IVs that seem to have been cannibalised for spare parts, including road wheels and drive sprockets. Operation Solstice, like the attacks in the Ardennes and in Hungary, achieved little other than to weaken the Waffen-SS even further and hasten the end of the war.